Dedication

To Rodney Nguyen – my friend, you are a true Miracle Alchemist; you have transmuted your pain into purpose. When you told me that my first book inspired you to write *You Khanh Do It*, you became my Miracle and my reminder that my life purpose as a Miracle-ologist has always been divinely guided and every pain and misery happened for a reason. I know The Universe connected us, that someday we'll meet in person, and we will walk and talk like old friends catching up as if it's just another day in our Miracle-licious lives!

Contents

Introduction

Why You Should Read This Book

This book was designed as a DONE-FOR-YOU MIRACLE STRATEGIES GUIDEBOOK.

Each chapter stands on its own and focuses ONLY on one Miracle Goal, so **you do not need to read the whole book to receive your Miracle Strategies and Guidance.** Simply look at the table of contents and choose the Miracle Goal you're wanting to achieve. These Goals vary in spiritual topics, from Miracle Guidance and Miracle Money to Life Purpose, Miracles For Loved Ones, and so much more!

Each chapter systematically guides you through four easy-to-follow steps so you are not left overwhelmed but rather knowing exactly what to do mentally, physically, and spiritually to help transform negative situations into Miracle opportunities to become the Miracle Alchemist you are meant to be!

I used to wish I had such a guidebook to follow during stressful times, when I most needed Miracles in my life. Then, after discovering my inner Miracle Alchemist, I decided to create that book for you, so you have crystal-clear guidance on the MIRACLE MINDSET THINK-ING needed to call in Miracles, seemingly without effort. That book, *Believe to Receive It: Activate the Miracles Waiting For You (2020)*, is a deep dive into the challenges I faced on all fronts and how I overcame them by shifting my mindset. *Believe It to Receive It* is based on an eight-week framework designed to help you get in the flow of calling in your Miracles, and shed any doubts that they are possible. Then I realized the need for a follow-up that teaches you to call in your Miracles even faster.

The Miracle Alchemist is based on the same foundation but follows an expedited process for "instant" Miracle manifesting. There is also an instant jolt of spirituality and MIRACLE STRATEGIES & GUIDANCE to guide you away from the fear-based thinking that can often block Miracle manifestation when you are feeling most desperate.

I truly believe that Miracles have their own energy. I speak to this energy as if it's my Dear Old Friend, asking it for Miracle guidance on manifestations (and anything and everything else) on a daily basis. After doing this for twenty-plus years, I know that Miracles speak back to all of us, in various ways, to help guide us to our Miracle solutions sooner. As with anything, if you do not communicate to Miracles or ask for guidance, they become silent and invisible and you don't notice them in your life. But the more you ask for insight and Miracles, the more you will notice their guidance and the more Miracles will appear in your life.

My hope is that this book helps you discover your own "Dear Old Friend," talk to it each day, and begin to feel this Miracle energy that is always around you. I can promise that if you follow the steps, you will more easily CALL IN or BE GUIDED TO YOUR MIRACLE SOLUTIONS TOO!

Please know this book was intentionally created with nonreligious references and ONLY BROAD INSPIRATIONAL TERMS, such as Higher Power, Higher Self, Angels and The Universe. This way, you can combine your own belief system with these Miracle ideas, strategies, and guidance.

The SECRET to Reading this Book

Miracle-Licious Suggestions to Alchemize Your Miracles Faster!

his book follows a simple, four-step outline to help you align your **Thoughts, Words, and Actions with your Intentions.** This won't take much thinking on your part, because the process has been STRATEGIZED and DONE FOR YOU. All you need to do in each chapter is integrate *Mind, Body, and Soul Intentions* with YOUR CHOSEN MIRACLE GOAL.

Here are some suggestions to keep in mind as you go through this process:

- I always suggest "plugging in" to your INNER GUIDANCE and/or HIGHER POWER before reading each chapter; this will help you stay on purpose and focused on your Miracle so you are guided to your Miracle solution ASAP. If you are not familiar with the term "plugging in," it is just my way of saying grounding yourself, praying, and visualizing to align yourself more consciously and unconsciously with your INNER GUID- ANCE and/or Higher Power. I personally do both – plugging in and talking to the MIRACLE ENERGY (my Dear Old Friend) that I believe is always surrounding each and every one of us. (If you want an in-depth example of plugging, check out Chapter

One of my first book, *Believe It to Receive It: Activate the Miracles Waiting For You.*

- Please understand that any time I use words like "issue," "situation," and "challenges," I'm doing so intentionally and instead of words like "problem," "illness," and "bankruptcy." This is because I truly believe that YOUR WORDS ARE YOUR WAND – you can use them to give more energy to certain situations or to take energy away from them. I personally choose to "deactivate" negative words, so I only think and talk about them as temporary situations and substitute them with more moderate words such as those mentioned above.

- While using this book for your Miracle Strategies Sessions, first find the chapter that fits your Miracle Goal in the table of contents, then follow the EASY OUTLINE THAT IS GIVEN WITH EACH MIRACLE CHAPTER. **Remember, while the outline is the same for every chapter, there is different Miracle content throughout the book.**

Here is the SECRET to make this book More Miracle-licious for you!

THE "BEGIN HERE" CHAPTER

This is the suggested starting point because it helps you discern whether you are receiving INNER GUIDANCE from your SOURCE ENERGY/HIGHER SELF or receiving FALSE GUIDANCE from your EGO, which slows down the manifestation of your Miracle. Also, this chapter helps you understand WHEN and IF any ACTION is needed that will take you toward your Miracle SOONER!

Each chapter has the following four steps, so here are some ideas to keep in mind.

1st STEP: MIRACLE TOOLS

This step is an example of the self-talk I have used to manifest Miracle Goals for myself in each chapter. I too need help to get my mindset upgraded energetically so I can truly believe my Miracle Goal is possible!

- **Refer to this step as often as needed while manifesting to keep your mindset programmed to the unlimited possibilities of your Miracles!**

2nd STEP: RELEASING

This section is to help you release any negative thinking, consciously or unconsciously, that could be slowing down the manifestation of your Miracle because It's NOT YOUR JOB TO FIND A MIRACLE SOLUTION!

- **Your number one priority is to release anything that could be blocking your Miracles. If you do this, your Higher Power and/or The Universe will take care of the rest!**

3rd STEP: CALL IN MIRACLES

I truly believe that the words you speak call in your future. In this section I give five ways to use *Words As Your Wand*. Find one or two phrases that feel aligned with you.

- **Repeat the Miracle Mantras like a broken record until you believe them with your mind, body, and soul. This belief alchemizes your energy and transforms your situation into your Miracles!**

4th STEP: ACTION ACCELERATOR

The previous steps involved using your thoughts and words to help alchemize your situations into manifesting your Miracles. In this last step, I show you how to use ACTIONS to communicate to the Miracle energy that surrounds you. These ACTIONS are those I HAVE PERSONALLY USED to ACTIVATE the energy around you in preparation for your Miracle, which is already here or will be any minute.

- **Remember, the more you believe in your Miracle mentally, physically, and spiritually, the faster your Miracle solution, designed just for you, will appear!**

FINALLY

Remember, you've already started the process of being guided to your Miracle because you were guided to this book. That was the first real step to your Miracle using your Inner Guidance.

- **Please know, without a doubt, that when you decided to make your Miracle life a priority, The Universe started collaborating to transform your situation into a divinely designed Miracle solution!**

Thank you for trusting me to help you with this journey to becoming a Miracle Alchemist and creating your Miracle-licious life!

Bernadette Rodebaugh

Begin Here

Receiving Crystal-Clear Miracle Guidance

*"The Miracles you are seeking are SEEKING YOU.
These Miracles are COMMUNICATING to YOU,
to GUIDE YOU to them SOONER!"*

When I was three years old, my mom took me for my check-up. The doctor asked her if she could understand what I was saying and Mom said that no, nobody could understand me.

He referred me to a speech therapist and, after many tests, they decided I had reversible brain damage. During the last trimester of my mother's pregnancy, she'd caught the Hong Kong flu; since she already had asthma, this flu affected her lungs. Her inability to breathe properly meant my brain did not get enough oxygen during the last stage of development, hence the reversible brain damage that affected my speech and ability to process thoughts and words properly.

My very first memory is of the speech therapist's office, with her playing games with me. Of course, at three years old, I thought we were just playing; now, I understand how she was helping me understand the world around me, interpret it correctly, and use words so I could communicate efficiently with others.

Now in my fifties, I understand the profound healing – physically, mentally, and emotionally – that began at that tender age. Most of all, I realize that my early experience of not being understood created a deep need within to understand others; it also gifted me with the ability to do so even when words are not used. I am extra intuitive of my surroundings, and I notice what is and what is not being said, unconsciously and consciously reading between the lines of the world around me. I am also more consciously aware when Miracles are communicating with me and how to interpret these messages.

Part of my life's mission is to share this information with you. That is not to say you won't find this information in other places. What I am saying is that because of my unique history and dedication to studying personalities and communication styles as an adult, I have simplified this process, and I believe that by the end of this chapter you will have this ability to communicate with your Miracles more easily too!

1st STEP: MIRACLE MINDSET

This is not merely positive thinking. This is MIRACLE MINDSET THINKING to help you SHIFT YOUR THINKING INTO TRULY BELIEVING YOUR MIRACLES ARE POSSIBLE!

> *"There are only two ways to live your life. One is as though nothing is a MIRACLE. The other is as though everything is a MIRACLE."*

> **-Albert Einstein**

I agree with Einstein wholeheartedly; in fact, I want you to keep his philosophy in mind as you learn how to tap into your MIRACLE GUIDANCE. Why? Because I truly believe that the more you expect a Miracle, the more Miracles will be revealed to you. That's the most fascinating thing about this: you won't just see the Miracle you were asking for, but other Miracles you didn't even know you wanted will start showing up as well!

I truly believe that Miracles have their own energy, and this energy communicates to you in your individual communication style.

I also refer to this "Miracle energy" as "Miracle Angels," so if at any time you have a hard time thinking of Miracles as an energy, you too can call them Miracle Angels, your Higher Power energy, or anything more aligned with your beliefs. There is no wrong way or right way – your Miracles will show up however you can believe in them. *What's important, first and foremost, is that you do believe in them.* Here are three of my favorite ways to get into this mindset when I am feeling reluctant or worried about my Miracle arriving and GUIDING ME.

Stepping into your MIRACLE MINDSET THINKING is kind of like deciding to step out of your current reality and into a world where

Miracles are possible. The idea is to Imagine in your mind until you feel that Miracles and MIRACLE GUIDANCE is real … or, at least, could be at any minute!

Close your eyes and imagine Miracle energy surrounding you, using one of the below examples. Make sure it feels good and/or in alignment with what you can believe in <u>currently</u>!

- At least 1000 heavenly "Miracle Angels" of all different sizes and glowing with different colors of the rainbow are encircling you and the room you are in. As they hug you, as you feel their deep, profound love healing you from the inside out. You begin to feel Heaven is on Earth.

- A beautiful, almost too bright white light from your Higher Power is surrounding you with so much love and compassion you feel like you have a thick, fluffy, warm blanket around you. As this light of love soothes all your fears and worries away, you now feel confident that your MIRACLE GUIDANCE is coming ASAP.

- An illuminating golden light of positive universal energy is now emanating from your heart center. With one deep breath, this light expands around you; with your next deep breath, it engulfs the room you're in; then, with one last deep breath, this light expands with lightning speed up to the heavens and down to the center of Earth. As it encompasses the whole world, you have a deep, profound, knowingness that the Miracles you are seeking are NOW coming to you easily and effortlessly. YOU HAVE BECOME A BEACON OF MIRACLE LIGHT CALLING THEM TOWARD YOU.

When you can imagine a Miracle presence is possible, or even if you can pretend to see it in your mind's eye with one of those examples above, you're ready to move on to the Next Step.

2ⁿᵈ STEP: RELEASING

This step is critical before you move onto the following steps because you need to RELEASE ANY BELIEF IN THE OPPOSITE OF THE MIRACLE YOU ARE ASKING FOR. Why? Because while YOUR HIGHER POWER AND/OR HIGHER SELF HAS UNLIMITED POSSIBLE MIRACLE SOLUTIONS, your belief (or lack thereof) can be blocking or slowing down their ability to intervene on your behalf.

Below, choose one or both AFFIRMATIONS to remind you that this situation is not your problem anymore. Then rewrite it below in the blank area until you have it memorized; this way you're confirming it to your conscious and unconscious mind.

- **I now choose to RELEASE…**

  All self-doubt, in any part of me that believes that Miracles are NOT communicating to me or that I need to be special or better in any way to receive MIRACLE GUIDANCE.

- **From this moment forward, I LET GO…**

  Of any negative thinking that separates me from believing I AM ONE WITH ALL POSITIVE UNIVERSAL ENERGY as it is guiding me to the MIRACLE-ICIOUS life I desire and deserve!

Before you turn the page repeat the following out loud…

"I NOW STEP INTO BEING THE MIRACLE ALCHEMIST
I came into this life to be!

AMEN, SO IT IS, THANK YOU!"

3rd STEP: CALL IN MIRACLE

This is a reminder that "WORDS TRULY ARE YOUR WAND," and when you speak you can CALL IN, COMMAND, CLAIM, BELIEVE, and use GRATITUDE to help create the Miracle future you want. Choose one or two MIRACLE MANTRAS below to repeat and think about often throughout every single day until your Miracle is here.

DOUBLE DOWN ON THIS whenever you are tempted to think and speak negatively or worry about anything that is opposite of the Miracle Solution you are wanting to manifest!

- **I NOW CALL IN...**

  Miracle Angels to guide me to my Miracle solutions. I now understand without a doubt my "Next Best Step" to receiving my Miracles easily and effortlessly.

- **I NOW COMMAND...**

  The Universe to surround me with love and light so that I easily understand every single message guiding me to my Miracle (healthier, happier, wealthier, loving) life!

- **I NOW CLAIM...**

  Miracles love me and I love Miracles! Miracles and I are one, so there is no misunderstanding as Miracles guide me instantly in every area of my life!

- **I NOW BELIEVE...**

  The Miracles I am seeking are seeking me. They are now guiding me exactly at the right moment at exactly the right time. I never miss a Miracle opportunity!

- **I AM SO THANKFUL...**

  That my Miracles guide me to every wish and desire I have ever wanted, from this moment forward!

REPEAT the following out loud…

*"THANK YOU, ALL POSITIVE UNIVERSAL ENERGY,
FOR HELPING ME CALL IN MY MIRACLES!"*

4th STEP: ACTION ACCELERATOR

Intentional ACTIONS that guide you to Activate The Energy of Allowing to become a MIRACLE ALCHEMIST!

BE AWARE:
This is the ONLY CHAPTER considered to be your PERSONAL ALCHEMIST MIRACLE REFERENCE GUIDE.

- This means you refer to this chapter anytime you've asked for a message from your Miracle and you're trying to decipher if you received a True MIRACLE GUIDANCE or false (egoic) guidance.

- IT IS THE ONLY CHAPTER that explains the ACTION that Miracles take to communicate to you! In the rest of the book, this section will be about you and your "ACTION STEP" to help you actualize your MIRACLE.

- IN THIS CHAPTER, YOUR ACTION STEP IS WHATEVER YOU ARE GUIDED TO DO AFTER YOU RECEIVE YOUR MIRACLE GUIDANCE. However, at the end of this chapter, you will do an "ACTION STEP" to help anchor in your MIRACLE GUIDANCE and give you the CONFIDENCE to follow through with the guidance steps that you receive.

THE FOLLOWING INFORMATION IS CRITICAL TO RECEIVING MIRACLE GUIDANCE:

I know, after twenty years of studying Miracles and asking for MIRACLE GUIDANCE daily, that every single Miracle answer I have ever received has always come through as a guided step to follow. When I take that step, the next step will show up, and so on, until my Miracle is here, which generally takes about three steps total.

If I don't take that first step, the next step does NOT show up, Therefore, it is imperative to act on the guidance immediately!

Being conscious of this guidance is important because it will come to each person differently. An easy way to think of this is that everyone has a natural communication style they were born with, and this is evident to you through your individual unique awareness and personal preferences.

To explain this, and simplify it even more, visualize the following exercise[1*]:

I want you to imagine that you go on a tropical vacation to Hawaii. You arrive in one of those private jets, the kind where you step right off the airplane onto the tarmac. As the flight crew unlocks and opens the airplane door, you descend a set of stairs that lead you down to the airplane apron, where you are met by an attractive Hawaiian woman with beautiful black, long wavy hair, olive-brown skin, and big, dark eyes. She greets you with, "Aloha," then, introducing herself as the hotel concierge, she places a lei of bright flowers around your neck.

You notice the gentle warm sun rays and a tropical, moist breeze that blows through your hair and across your skin with a delightful, sweet fragrance of Hawaiian flowers. Suddenly, you hear in the distance a ukulele playing a Hawaiian song you've never heard before. You're in paradise, and as you walk toward the airport entryway, you're thinking, "What type of career would I need to do to live here permanently?"

---

[*] This is paraphrased from Doreen Virtue's 1999 book, *Divine Guidance: How to Have a Dialogue with God and Your Guardian Angels.* Twenty years ago, when I attended one of her trainings, Virtue said we were welcome to use any of her information to teach others. Please note that since then she has renounced any connection to all things metaphysical and ceased publication of her metaphysical/New Age books.

Now take a moment and think about the above description. Then choose and circle 1 or 2 items below <u>that stood out in your mind the MOST.</u>

A= The site of the attractive Hawaiian concierge.

B = The feeling of the wind and sun on your skin.

C =The sound of the Hawaiian ukulele music.

D= Thoughts about looking for a job so that you can stay on this island.

These four choices are examples of your natural awareness of what you see, feel, hear, and know; what you choose reflects the communication style you were born with and what I refer to as your MIRACLE language preference. Another way to explain this is your intuition ability or the four "claires," which I explain below, along with the description of what each of the above choices represents.

This information will give you an idea of what you naturally are aware of without much thought, because when Miracles communicate to you, the information comes through the same natural process of your awareness and unique discernment. In other words, you're now going to be more *consciously* guided by your natural *unconscious* abilities.

DESCRIPTION EXAMPLES:

Be sure to read all the letters, because the more you connect with your intuitive MIRACLE GUIDANCE the more information will start showing up in the other communication styles that you may not have noticed previously. Keep in mind that this is just an introduction to communication styles. The more you use the information in this book, the clearer your exact preferences for Miracles to communicate to you will be.

A= Clairvoyance (clear seeing)
This GUIDANCE will appear as pictures in your mind or future movies in your head. These thoughts appear out of nowhere.

B= Clairsentience (clear feeling)

This GUIDANCE shows up as feelings on your body. This can be good feelings, such as butterflies in your stomach or hair standing up on your skin, or bad feelings you may experience around certain people, places, or things.

C= Clairaudience (clear hearing)

This GUIDANCE will appear as voices (yours or another's) that you hear in your head. Some people believe this is their higher power, higher self, or angels talking to them. This information *is always* positive; it will never make you feel bad and certainly will never tell you to do anything to hurt yourself or others.

D= Claircognizance (clear knowing)

This GUIDANCE appears as a knowing of something as fact. You may not always know *how* you know – it's like a download of information or ideas that just come to you out of nowhere – but you know it without a doubt.

To help confirm that you are ready to receive your MIRACLE GUID-ANCE, repeat the following MIRACLE MANTRA:

"Miracles guide me in every area of my life. I NOW see, hear, feel, and know my NEXT BEST STEP TO MY MIRACLE SOLUTION WITHOUT A DOUBT."

The most fascinating thing for me when learning about this information was the correlation between your four claires and your preferred communication style when interacting with people. This understanding made me very successful as a hairstylist, because within five minutes of meeting someone I could figure out their preferred communication style and then communicate almost effortlessly with them in that style. This helped them relax instantly, and as my clairsentience wasn't picking up on any stress or worry about their hair, we were both more at ease and could enjoy the appointment!

Honestly, I could go on and on about this information and how to use it in every area of your life, because it has been an absolute game-changer for me. I now have more peace and harmony in my daily life, and other people's personalities and/or communication styles no longer rub me the wrong way because I realize nothing they do has anything to do with me. Most importantly, I KNOW WITHOUT A DOUBT when I'm receiving communication from Miracles, my angels, and The Universe that surround me.

NOTE:

If you want more in-depth understanding of the four claires and other MIRACLE-accelerating tips, I created a course that focuses specifically on that. The link is below and you will get a half-off discount, just because you read this book!

themiracle-school.com/p/miracle-accelerator?coupon_code=MIRACLES

ACTION STEP

To feel more confident and connected to your MIRACLE GUIDANCE, try the following whenever possible throughout your day.

- The next time the phone rings, the doorbell rings, or you receive a text, close your eyes and ask your MIRACLE guidance, "Who is that contacting me?" or "What is this call about?"

  Wait and see if you receive a picture in your mind or hear a voice in your head, a feeling in your body, or a knowingness of who it is without knowing *how* you know.

- Use oracle cards, such as the "Activate Your MIRACLE Guidance" cards I created. As you shuffle or mix up the cards, ask a question, and wait until one of your four claires tells you which card to flip over. Here are some of the ways this can happen:
- HEARING "Stop now," or something similar.
- FEELING the cards and noticing that one feels "better" than the others.
- LOOKING at the cards and noticing that one seems brighter or has a different hue.
- KNOWING which card to grab.

Then, before you flip it over, ask yourself if you know what color, words, general topic, or meaning is on the other side of the card, waiting to be revealed to you.

By taking these everyday opportunities, you can start to become more attuned to the MIRACLE messages that surround you and are guiding you every minute of every day.

FYI, if you are wanting to practice with my Activate Your MIRACLE Guidance cards, here is the link:

themiracle-ologist.com

BONUS STEP

Here are some ideas on how to be more MIRACLE-LICIOUS and SEAL THE DEAL TO LOCK IN YOUR MIRACLE ALCHEMY!

Allow at least 15 minutes for the following process. Don't forget to plug into your Inner Guidance first. In addition to writing it, read the following out loud (remember, you're speaking to the energy that surrounds you) while calling in your Miracles.

"Dear MIRACLE Energy that surrounds me, I now give you permission to communicate to me

with crystal clear guidance using my hearing, feeling, knowing, and seeing abilities. I trust you to guide me without a doubt to my Next Best Step toward my MIRACLE_____. (fill in.)

From this moment forward, I am committing myself to being aware of you and your guidance that surrounds me, as I truly want to be a MIRACLE ALCHE-MIST AS YOU GUIDE ME TO TRANSFORM MY LIFE, TO THE MIR-ACLE LIFE, THAT I DESERVE AND AM NOW CALLING FORTH!

I trust you to let me know if there is anything else I need to do to deepen this communication and understanding between us."

Sign your FULL NAME below, as this is your bond and commitment, physically and spiritually. To, YOUR NEW MIRACLE LIFE!

_____.

Now take a moment to think, and then write about *at least one* (more is great) "MIRACLE MOMENT," when you seemed to be in the right place at just the right moment. Anything that seemed like "the moon and stars were aligned just for you." Why do we do this? Because remembering Miracle moments that have already happened will help you receive more Miracle moments.

_____

_____

_____

_____

_____

_____

_____

_____

_____

_____

_____

_____

_____

_____

Miracle Goal

Activate Your Miracle Mindset

*M*iracle thinking is NOT the same as positive thinking… it is MIRACLE MINDSET THINKING!

It is the ability to look at the reality that surrounds you and say to yourself, "*This is no longer my truth. My truth is Miracles exist, and there is a Miracle solution for this situation, and I trust that MY MIRACLE ANSWER IS NOW GUIDED TO ME EASILY AND EFFORTLESSLY.*

During this time of activating your "MIRACLE MINDSET," you may need a thicker skin and not allow the small thinking of the physical world to bother you; this world is not focused on Miracles, and you will be.

This will also be a time to keep reminding yourself that you do not need to know EXACTLY HOW EVERYTHING WILL WORK OUT. Why? Because there are INFINITE POSSIBILITIES and MIRACLE SOLUTIONS TO EVERY SITUATION!

Let's begin with ACTIVATING this truth out loud to YOU and YOUR HIGHER SELF, on all levels, by repeating the following:

"I_____ *(fill in your full name)*

- *Declare that I do not need to KNOW, UNDERSTAND, or HAVE ALL THE ANSWERS, for my life or for this world.*
- *Know that I ONLY need to ACCEPT that there is a MIRACLE SOLUTION TO EVERY SITUATION, and I have no need to completely comprehend the extent of these solutions at this moment.*
- *NOW choose to BELIEVE AND TRUST THAT THE UNIVERSE IS WORKING FOR ME and NOT AGAINST ME.*
- *Did NOT come into this life to have prolonged unhealthiness in any area of my life – personally, professionally, mentally, physically, financially, or spiritually.*
- *"Am living and breathing MIRACLE THINKING. This is who I AM. I allow Miracles to work through me, around me, for me in every area of my and my family's life."*
- *AFFIRM THAT I AM NOW A miracle, believer, and allower, knowing that this is truly how I STEP INTO THE NEW ME… THE MIRACLE ALCHEMIST MANIFESTOR!"*

To embrace this MIRACLE MINDSET thinking, you must absolutely become purely focused on ALLOWING THE MIRACLE SOLUTIONS to be revealed to you, INSTEAD OF TRYING TO FIGURE OUT the Miracle solution you see fit!

Whenever you are wanting or needing to manifest a Miracle, go into that sacred place in your mind, heart, and soul that believes in Miracles. To help with this process, surround yourself with ONLY POSITIVE MIRACLE ENERGY. This means that everything you NOW DO, THINK, TALK, ABOUT, or ALLOW in your physical presence is only of the highest vibration of POSITIVITY and MIRACLE-NESS!

Be aware that during this time the circle of family and friends that surround you may become smaller and more intimate. Don't let this bother you. Not everybody can handle the high vibes of Miracle energy that you're going to be embodying, BECAUSE YOU WILL BE INFUSING YOUR LIFE WITH ONLY POSITIVITY for A MIRACLE-ENABLING ENVIRONMENT.

The Law of Attraction, which states that "like is attracted to like," is put into motion by something I like to call "THE LAW OF MIRACLES." This means that TO RECEIVE MIRACLES, YOU MUST BE LIVING AND BREATHING MIRACLE THINKING! You become the "Law of Attraction in Action" by creating an inner environment that lives and breathes Miracles, which then radiates from the inside out as a vibration that NOW ATTRACTS MIRACLES TO YOU!

This is a time for you to put yourself and your MIRACLE FIRST, UNAPOLOGETICALLY, as if your life depends on it. Why? Because your Miracle life *does* depend on it!

I remember the first time I made this kind of thinking and being a priority in my life. I had this best friend, and we enjoyed talking to each other on the phone every morning while we were getting ready for our day. The problem was, all we talked about was how horrible our husbands were and, to make matters worse, my husband and I were talking about divorce. Then I learned about the power of "like attracts like" and realized that the more I complained about my husband, the more things to complain about showed up! Not only was complaining *not* making me feel better, it was making the circumstances in my marriage worse.

So, I said to this best friend ...

"Hey, I'm trying to improve and work on my marriage, so I'm not going to talk negatively about my husband anymore."

I went on to explain to her what I had learned about the Law of Attraction – that the more we complain about something, the more we'll find to complain about.

I then suggested...

"We should be talking about is all the wonderful things our husbands do, then we will find more wonderful things about them to talk about."

I then said...

"I will go first to start the conversation..."

I don't remember what I said next, but I do remember she suddenly didn't have time to talk and rushed me off the phone. Within a month she was no longer returning my calls.

At first I was devastated and wondering what I could have done to this friend that upset her so much. As time went on, my husband and I began to heal our marriage and fall back in love with each other. (I talk about this in more detail later on.) The interesting thing is that about a year later this same friend suddenly wanted to meet me for lunch. She asked me for forgiveness, though she also said she didn't know what she had done to me. She wondered, what had happened to our friendship? I told her it was nothing I could specifically remember, because I truly had forgotten about it!

Later, as I was thinking about the conversation, I realized how much my energy had changed; truly, I was no longer the same person who had related to her – no matter that she was the one who pushed our friendship aside. I knew it wasn't worth pointing fingers, because....

"Vibrationally, this is how divine intervention of the Law of Attraction' works."

This is an example of how, when you start raising your vibration and being energetically healthier and happier in all areas in your life, circumstances or people will be gently released from your life. You are no longer "alike" or vibing with one another anymore.

This is nobody's fault, it's just …

> *"A Miracle solution to your situation, that you had no idea would be a CATALYST FOR THE MIRACLE you've been asking for."*

Now that you understand the importance of making yourself and your Miracle a priority, let's take this a step further so that you can TRULY EMBRACE LIVING AND BREATHING MIRACLE MINDSET THINKING!

As mentioned, this is the only chapter in which having a MIRACLE MINDSET is your MIRACLE GOAL. This will help you prepare for all your other MIRACLE GOALS in the rest of this book, so that you can TRULY BE A MIRACLE ALCHEMIST!

1ˢᵗ STEP: MIRACLE MINDSET

This is not merely positive thinking. This is MIRACLE MINDSET THINKING to help you SHIFT YOUR THINKING INTO TRULY BELIEVING YOUR MIRACLES ARE POSSIBLE!

The magic of truly believing in Miracles is the ability to see and imagine your Miracle, knowing it is here now, or will be at any minute. With this kind of focus on Miracle thinking, you truly call your Miracle to you! Some might say you are magical because your future brings you exactly what you want – or even better!

However, you know you are just a normal, everyday person who said, "I want more of this and less of that …" regarding whatever was available to you at that moment.

With this belief in your Miracle you automatically become Miracle-licious … YES, DELICIOUS TO MIRACLES. By this I mean it will seem that Miracles search for you instead of the other way around.

Others are wondering what your secret is, but you know you just decided to think and talk ONLY about what you want to be TRUE. Then you envisioned it, which helps you believe in it before you can see it, BECAUSE YOU KNOW YOU CAME HERE TO BE A MIRACLE CREATOR OF YOUR DESTINY, a.k.a. A MIRACLE ALCHEMIST!

> **Decide right now that you are done living a mediocre life and you're ready for your Miracle life. Confirm this decision by going to the next step.**

2nd STEP: RELEASING

This step is critical before you move onto the following steps because you need to RELEASE ANY BELIEF IN THE OPPOSITE OF THE MIRACLE YOU ARE ASKING FOR. Why? Because while YOUR HIGHER POWER AND/OR HIGHER SELF HAS UNLIMITED POSSIBLE MIRACLE SOLUTIONS, your belief (or lack thereof) can be blocking or slowing down their ability to intervene on your behalf.

Below, choose one or both AFFIRMATIONS to remind you that this situation is not your problem anymore. Then rewrite it below in the blank area until you have it memorized; this way you're confirming it to your conscious and unconscious mind.

- **I NOW choose to RELEASE…**

  Every thought and feeling that reflects the belief that I couldn't have every Miracle I've ever wanted to manifest!

- **From this moment forward, I LET GO**

  Of the small version of myself that played small in this game of life and thought of myself in lack or without my Miracle.

Before you turn the page, repeat the following out loud …

"I NOW STEP INTO BEING THE MIRACLE ALCHEMIST
I came into this life to be!

AMEN, SO IT IS, THANK YOU!"

3ʳᵈ STEP: CALL IN MIRACLE

This is a reminder that "WORDS TRULY ARE YOUR WAND," and when you speak you can CALL IN, COMMAND, CLAIM, BELIEVE, and use GRATITUDE to help create the Miracle future you want. Choose one or two MIRACLE MANTRAS below to repeat and think about often throughout <u>every single day until your Miracle is here.</u>

DOUBLE DOWN ON THIS whenever you're tempted to think or speak negatively or worry about anything that is opposite of the Miracle Solution you are wanting to manifest!

- **I NOW CALL IN…**

  My Higher Self for divine intervention to alchemize my current mediocre thinking and transmute it to Miracle Thinking for my New Improved Miracle Life!

- **I NOW COMMAND…**

  From this moment forward, I choose to live a life full of MIRACLES, wherever I go, whatever I'm doing, Miracles surround me, guide me, and protect me!

- **I NOW CLAIM…**

  The Universe fulfills every Miracle wish I Dare to Dream!

- **I NOW BELIEVE…**

  My Miracle Angels are here to help and guide me easily and effortlessly to the most Miracle-Filled Life I can imagine!

- **I AM SO THANKFUL…**

  That I live, breathe, and ONLY THINK about MIRACLES because MIRACLE MANIFESTOR is Who I Am!

REPEAT the following out loud:

*"THANK YOU, ALL POSITIVE UNIVERSAL ENERGY,
FOR HELPING ME CALL IN MY MIRACLES!"*

4th STEP: ACTION ACCELERATOR

Intentional ACTIONS that guide you to <u>Activate The Energy Of Allowing</u> to become a MIRACLE ALCHEMIST!

Remember, MIRACLE MINDSET is living and breathing your Miracle as if it's here, NOW...NO MATTER WHAT the outside circumstances look like! This fun exercise is to help you step into the world where your Miracle lives so you can believe in them more and raise your vibration to allow the Miracle to find you sooner!

ACTION STEP

ALLOW AT LEAST 15 MINUTES FOR THIS.

FIND A BLANK PAGE IN THE JOURNAL SECTION AT THE BACK OF THIS BOOK AND JOURNAL THE FOLLOWING.

1: Imagine...
Opening your front door, and – BOOM! – INSTANTLY, YOUR MIRACLE IS THERE. It has been delivered to you!

Close your eyes if you need to and completely 100% imagine living and breathing your Miracle as if it's alive and in your hands, right NOW as a part of your life and who you are.

2: Write...
Dear_____, (fill in your Higher Power/Higher Self or Angels)

I'M SO THANKFUL THAT TODAY WHEN I OPENED MY FRONT DOOR – BOOM! – MY MIRACLE INSTANTLY ARRIVED!

- Imagine all the good feelings and relief that wash over your body, from head to toe, with the electric feeling of Miracle energy – because your Miracle solution has arrived!

- Write what this looks, feels, smells, and tastes like. Describe how your life is so much different and better now that your Miracle is here.

- Write what your family and friends say when you tell them your Miracle has arrived.

- What is your next step? Do you throw a celebration party? Take everybody on vacation?

Keep in mind that whatever you write about should feel Exhilarating and Miracle-licious!

Reread this as much as possible, especially when you're needing to BELIEVE IN YOUR MIRACLE THE MOST!

BONUS STEP

Here are some ideas on how to be more MIRACLE-LICIOUS and SEAL THE DEAL TO LOCK IN YOUR MIRACLE ALCHEMY!

What I'm about to suggest is ONLY FOR THE TRUE MIRACLE ALCHEMIST AND BELIEVER IN MIRACLES. It is for those who believe they can be a conscious creator of their life, including rewriting a specific part of their SOUL CONTRACT that may not currently be reflecting the level to which they have spiritually evolved and want their life to represent. Here's a personal example: I believe I'm a healer whose life purpose has been to help others with their healing. The problem was, even though I was guided to various healings in my life, then spoke or wrote books to help others with their own healings, I still often found myself with one life or health challenge after another… UNTIL I DECIDED I no longer wished to experience challenges to overcome so I could then teach others the tools I'd learned. So one day I decided to rewrite my soul contract from being the archetype of being a wounded healer, *which means one who has been wounded and then teaches others to heal. I NOW CLAIM I AM A HEALED HEALER* who no longer needs to experience illness or other challenges to help others! To me this means I am still in alignment with my life purpose **but now I no longer choose or allow situations in my life that need astronomical healings!**

This stems from the belief in "ASK AND IT IS GIVEN; SEEK AND YOU SHALL RECEIVE." As far as I'm concerned, this has nothing to do with religion; it's really about your belief that you were not created to have a miserable life or remain stuck in certain negative situations forever. Basically, these situations include anything that keeps you from being happy, and productive in your daily life and or on your life purpose.

This is the step I do when I'm going through something and am at the end of my rope; and I'm feeling mentally, physically, and spiritually exhausted from the situation or like I'm going in circles, experiencing the same issue over and over again; when I don't understood why my Higher Self has allowed the situation as a life lesson again, even when I understand the profound message but haven't been able to spiritually evolve past a certain point, I do the following process.

This is powerful, so before proceeding make sure you truly want to transmute a current situation AND that you're ready to evolve to whatever degree is needed – mentally, physically, and spiritually to be done with a certain soul or life lesson and you're ready to move on, toward your highest path and purpose for this lifetime

If this feels in alignment with you, go onto the next part.

ALLOW AT LEAST 15 MINUTES.

Don't forget to plug in and get connected to Source energy.

Fill in the following information while reading it out loud to lock it in better, consciously and unconsciously.

I'm calling forth my Higher Power, my Higher Self, and ALL POSITIVE UNIVERSAL ENERGY, including my personal spirit team of angels, teachers, masters, and guides, to surround me and guide me on my behalf from this moment forward, helping me with this situation around allowing my Miracle resolution and the conclusion of this issue to be transmuted to a Miracle solution, ASAP!

I BELIEVE that "Ask and You Shall Receive," and I NOW ASK with my whole heart and soul for CRYSTAL-CLEAR MIRACLE GUIDANCE and DIVINE INTERVENTION for the following situation: _____
_____. (fill in)

Because I DECLARE right NOW, at this moment to my Creator and Higher Self, and ALL POSITIVE UNIVERSAL ENERGY that I no longer allow, intend, or agree in this lifetime to be influenced with this issue of_____ (fill in) and any other related problems, anymore!

I NOW COMMAND for immediate positive resolution of the situation, and I am confirming that I am expecting a Miracle solution, such as the following or better, but NOT LIMITED by any means.

(Choose and circle one or more of the following or create your own conclusion.)

- Miracle healing in all areas of my life
- My Divine destiny now manifesting
- Prosperity (immediate infusion)
- A Divine and perfect peaceful ending to this situation

- Complete financial support from the Universe
- Everlasting, true love
- My Divine and ideal perfect career
- Complete healing in my mind, body, soul, and affairs
- Receiving my soulmate
- Or_____

I NOW TRUST, BELIEVE, AND HAVE FAITH THAT A DIVINE INTERVENTION HAS TAKEN PLACE, AND SO IT IS!

I now no longer need to think or wonder about this situation because it is done.

From this moment forward, I know my Miracle solution will show up within the next 30 days.

TODAY'S DATE_____.

THIRTY DAYS FROM NOW, THE DATE IS_____.

Thank You, Higher Power, and All Positive Universal Forces, including my personal Spirit Team, for this Divine intervention and complete trans-mutation of this Miracle life I have called forth today!

_____ (Fill in your complete name.)

Miracle Goal

Miracles For Loved Ones

*H*ave you ever wanted or wished a loved one would take better care of themselves, give up an addiction, become healthier, or step into the purposeful potential you know is inside them? This is even more complicated, exhausting, and overwhelming when that loved one has an illness that you can't control or isn't even being controlled medically!

This chapter's focus is how to help loved ones in challenging situations while honoring their free will and their Higher Selves' intentions for this lifetime – and NOT giving additional energy to the negativity in their life.

Something to keep in mind as you read this chapter: your thoughts are powerful and can create an unspoken energetic contribution, consciously and unconsciously, to the situation because…

When your loved one is going through a difficult situation or challenge in their life, you worry, obsess and/or try to control the situation. This can add more energy to the negativity of the issue; in other words, you're feeding it, which can empower it to grow and intensify. Your prayers and good intentions are being canceled out by your underlining FEAR, which in an odd way becomes its own prayer… for what you DON'T want to happen…TO HAPPEN!

I call this the fearful, self-fulfilling prophecy "prayer."

Gentle reminder: When you are thinking or talking about your loved one, always make sure it's filled with POSITIVE MIRACLE INTENTIONS instead of fear, because otherwise you're negatively adding to their situation instead of helping them. A simple way to think about this is...

"What you think about you bring about."

-Bob Proctor

Before we talk about the different ways you can positively help your loved ones with Miracles, we're first going to talk about you. Don't skip ahead, because this is very important and most likely will shine light on this situation, hopefully, like you've never seen it before.

Answer the following four questions. Just for clarification, these questions are not about you and your involvement with somebody else, like a relationship or a situation at your work. They are ONLY ABOUT YOU, individually.

1st

What is the number one thing you wish was improved or more ideal (basically, more perfect) about yourself or your life? When you realize exactly what that is, move to the next question.

2nd

Count how many times you have THOUGHT ABOUT THIS INTENTION to improve this situation or challenge about yourself? Come up with an actual number in your head before moving on.

3rd

Now that you realize one major thing about yourself that you'd like to improve or have had the intention to improve, I want you to come up with an exact number of times you've ACTUALLY TRIED WORKING ON THIS ISSUE. This means actual actions or steps taken toward your goal.

4th

Now that you have examined your own life, can you admit that even when you're inspired, motivated, and want to change or improve something about yourself, it's not an easy feat and takes **100% dedication and will from YOUR mind, body, and soul and, sometimes, a MIRACLE?**

Before I understood HOW TO BE A "MIRACLE ALCHEMIST," when trying to make any real improvements in my life I would make a dozen or more attempts (and, at some points, emotionally give up) before I actually changed my bad habit to a healthier one. The thing is, if friends or family made suggestions to me about the same intention, it worked like reverse psychology, actually "SHUT OFF" MY POSITIVE INTENTIONS BECAUSE, I HATE TO BE TOLD WHAT TO DO! All of this is to say how easy it is for us to get off course when trying to make positive changes in their life – and how unreasonable it is to expect others to make changes if they're not completely **100% inspired, dedicated, and so on!**

One last thing to keep in mind before you move on is that when our prayers are for somebody else, we don't always completely consider what that person truly wants, in their heart and soul, or AS THEIR HIGHER SELF.

This means that if the person we're praying for is going through a health challenge and they are truly tired and their Higher Self (or soul) is ready to return to their Maker, there's nothing we can do to change that situation. Our prayers of love and support, no matter how powerful, do not override their soul's true desire.

BUT if this person we're praying for decides, on a soul level, that they are ready to make the changes needed to live more in alignment with whatever their highest path and purpose is for this lifetime, their illness or challenge could be just a stepping stone in their new direction. Then you can truly help, energetically, on a spiritual level. These steps can also help someone you're praying for remember who their Higher Self is, and who they came here to be, which will help them realign themselves in the direction of their highest good (again, if they're Higher Self so wishes.)

Next, we will talk about how your thoughts and actions can Miraculously help your loved one truly be MORE MIRACLE-LICIOUS during challenging times!

1ˢᵗ STEP: MIRACLE MINDSET

This section is not merely positive thinking. This is MIRACLE MINDSET THINKING to help you SHIFT YOUR THINKING INTO TRULY BELIEVING YOUR MIRACLES ARE POSSIBLE!

Say the following, OUT LOUD:

"Today, at this moment, I remind myself that the best way for me to contribute to the Miracle of this situation is to be an example of unconditional love. This means every time I think of this person, it will be with loving, healthy thoughts of them, in every area of their life – mentally, physically, and spiritually.

Every time I talk to this person, or talk with someone else about this person, it will be with believing energy that their Miracle is complete. Because I know the power of believing in a Miracle before the eyes can see it is, in fact, often the catalyst for manifesting a Miracle.

I know the more I think about, talk about, and believe in this Miracle for my loved one's healthy life, the more contagious it will become to everyone involved, because this is the power of believing in Miracles and this is how the Alchemist breathes life into their Miracles!"

> **Next, we're going to begin by releasing any need to help carry the burdens of your loved one's situation. Seeing them as unable to carry their own burdens is not seeing them in their Higher Selves abilities, and this does not empower them.**

2nd STEP: RELEASING

This step is critical before you move onto the following steps because you need to RELEASE ANY BELIEF IN THE OPPOSITE OF THE MIRACLE YOU ARE ASKING FOR. Why? Because while YOUR HIGHER POWER AND/OR HIGHER SELF HAS UNLIMITED POSSIBLE MIRACLE SOLUTIONS, your belief (or lack thereof) can be blocking or slowing down their ability to intervene on your behalf.

Below, choose one or both AFFIRMATIONS to remind you that this situation is not your problem anymore. Then rewrite it below in the blank area until you have it memorized; this way you're confirming it to your conscious and unconscious mind.

- **I NOW choose to RELEASE…**

  Fear and worry about my loved one's challenges and issues. Because I know if I hold onto the idea that this is a problem in their life, I am giving energy to the problem.

- **From this moment forward, I LET GO…**

  Of my limited point of view of how I believe this situation should look, feel, or be.

Before you turn the page, repeat the following out loud:

*"I NOW STEP INTO BEING THE MIRACLE ALCHEMIST
I came into this life to be!*

AMEN, SO IT IS, THANK YOU!"

3rd STEP: CALL IN MIRACLE

This is a reminder that "WORDS TRULY ARE YOUR WAND," and when you speak you can CALL IN, COMMAND, CLAIM, BELIEVE, and use GRATITUDE to help create the Miracle future you want. Choose one or two MIRACLE MANTRAS below to repeat and think about often throughout <u>every day until your Miracle is here.</u>

DOUBLE DOWN ON THIS whenever you are tempted to think and speak negatively or worry about anything that is opposite of the Miracle Solution you are wanting to manifest!

- **I NOW CALL IN …**

  Miracle angels to surround my loved one and their situation while protecting them and guiding them to their MIRACLE SOLUTION!

- **I NOW COMMAND…**

  The Universe to transform my loved one's situation into a Miracle outcome that is BETTER than anything we can currently see, know, or understand!

- **I NOW CLAIM…**

  This situation_____ (fill in) has now been transformed Miraculously into a happily- ever-after Miracle story!

- **I NOW BELIEVE…**

  There is a Miracle solution to this situation, and my loved one NOW allows it to come to pass!

- **I AM SO GRATEFUL…**

  That Miracles NOW SURROUND MY LOVED ONE, and I no longer need to worry!

REPEAT the following out loud:

*"THANK YOU, ALL POSITIVE UNIVERSAL ENERGY,
FOR HELPING ME CALL IN MY MIRACLES!"*

4th STEP: ACTION ACCELERATOR

Intentional ACTIONS that guide you to Activate The Energy of Allowing to become a MIRACLE ALCHEMIST!

This is an empowering visualization that acts like a Miracle magnet for your loved one. It helps empower them with a higher vibrational energy sent with love from you to them. Think of this every time you're worried about your loved one and you're wanting to RELEASE OWNERSHIP of this situation.

ACTION STEP

ALLOW AT LEAST 5 MINUTES

- Close your eyes; imagine your loved one and their situation.

- Now, think about how much love you have for this person. Imagine this love is in the form of a beautiful, glowing pink light in the center of your heart space.

- Take three big deep breaths. Imagine with each inhale that this beautiful light becomes magnified, more powerful, and filled with MIRACLE ENERGY and/or MIRACLE ANGELS. Imagine this light growing until it overcomes your whole body and surrounds the room you're in, like a bubble of Miracle pink light.

- Now, take one last deep breath and imagine this beautiful bubble of Miracle light has EXPANDED and MIRACULOUSLY NOW SURROUNDS YOUR LOVED ONE AND THEIR SITUATION with love and protection.

- Imagine this "Miracle bubble" is now very gently lifting them up energetically, mentally, physically, spiritually, and financially, so they are healthier, and happier in every area of their life.

- They can now feel this deep, profound love from you, The Universe, their Higher Power, and their HIGHER SELF.

- This powerful energy is like a hot air balloon, lifting them up so they can connect with their MIRACLE SOURCE ENERGY, where all Miracle solutions surround them. They are now guided to their MIRACLE SOLUTION easily and effortlessly because of YOUR INTENTIONS OF LOVE, PROTECTION, AND MIRACLE GUIDANCE!

- NOW, WITH A GRATEFUL HEART, go about your day knowing that Miracles surround your loved ones, and you do not need to pray or think about this situation anymore!

- Trust that if there's anything for you to do, you'll be guided from a place of Divine love, not from fear!

BONUS STEP

Here are some ideas on how to be more MIRACLE-LICIOUS and SEAL THE DEAL TO LOCK IN YOUR MIRACLE ALCHEMY!

- Give your loved one a picture of both of you.

  The following is especially important. If your loved one is going through a health challenge or addiction, they likely don't see themselves as healed and beautiful, as you see them through your eyes. If this is the case, find the best picture you can of both of you that represents a time in their life when they were healthiest – mentally, physically, or spiritually. This could even be a picture from their childhood. Don't limit your ideas; ask for Miracle guidance and see what ideas come to you!

- Don't forget to be creative and fun. This could be a poster-size photo of both of you or a decorative frame you create just for them, or any idea that may help them smile when they're looking at it during this challenging time.

- Write the following or something similar, as a heading or a note on the backside:

  "I love you, and I BELIEVE IN YOUR MIRACLE, and so you don't feel alone during this challenging time, I'm giving you this picture to remind you that you are always on my mind and in my heart. I trust and believe you'll be guided to your MIRACLE SOLUTION. In the meantime, I'll keep praying for you, knowing soon you will be able to tell me all about your happily-ever-after Miracle story!

Miracle Goal

Fearlessness Is Your Superpower

*B*eing fearless is a superpower that nobody talks about. I know that when I first embraced the concepts of this chapter, I truly felt unstoppable and became the superwoman that I always dreamed I could be, because I had suddenly decided that I had...

> *The ability to look FEAR in the eyes and say,*
> *"Fuck you or forget you!"*

Truly, it is whatever you are more in alignment with at that moment, or whatever will empower you the most!

FEAR disguises itself as:

- **F**amily or Friends
- **E**veryone
- **A**nything
- **R**eality

Fear comes in many shapes and sizes. Sometimes it's your current reality of a medical diagnosis, your negative bank balance, or the news channel that tells you to expect only the worst possibilities of the world around you. Sometimes it is friends or family who think they have your best interest at heart but, really, their version of "your best interest" is FEAR camouflaged as concern and their version makes you feel hopeless unless you follow their suggestions.

> *"FEAR is anyone or anything that makes*
> *you doubt the possibility that a*
> ***MIRACLE SOLUTION IS YOUR ANSWER!"***

The goal of this chapter is to help you release all outside worries and concerns, to allow yourself to step into your Inner Guidance, where you can be guided to your Miracle Solution. This can be a person you meet, something you read, or information "accidentally" found on your social media. Google has brought me information I needed, which I then took to a doctor (when guided) for input to expedite the healing; I've even had epiphanies that certain types of food were not agreeing with my body, made those corrections, and – BOOM! – MY MIRACLE HEALING STARTS!

Once I realize the cause of my problem, I am then able to work on it mentally, physically, or spiritually to get to the root of the problem so it does not recur.

Remember, Miracles have an INFINITE NUMBER OF POSSIBILITIES and DIFFERENT WAYS TO SHOW UP, so don't judge any guidance you are receiving because it's not "practical." FOLLOW IT ANYWAY.

Most likely, your Miracle Solution will come unexpectedly and you know *without a doubt* that this information is your answer. You know this is the answer because you feel hope and inspired with an energy of excitement times a million, as if you're "lit up and electrified" in a good way, on a soul level!

For me, this feels like the inner guiding light in my heart center, as if it's lit from the inside out. It is a feeling of a tingling electrical alignment from Heaven and Earth coming together in my body. I feel both grounded and connected – and optimistic about my Miracle outcome.

I hope that description got you excited, because just imagining the above scenario and pretending that my Miracle has come to me with that "lit-up electricity feeling" has, BY ITSELF, been a catalyst for my Miracle to come sooner, even before I have received the actual message that it's on its way!

RIGHT NOW, TRY IMAGINING THAT MIRACLE FEELING.

Breathe it in. Pretend it's real at this moment. Imagine you can feel that "lit-up electricity feeling" connecting you to Heaven and Earth. Then truly believe it's possible, because connecting to that feeling is reminding your mind, body, and soul what a Miracle feels like so you can…

TRANSMUTE YOUR SITUATION INTO A MIRACLE!

> *"Just like an alchemist transforms everyday material things into gold or other treasures, YOU ARE NOW TRANSFORMING THOUGHTS, FEELINGS, AND IDEAS INTO DELICIOUS, MIRACLE-LICIOUS, LIFE-CHANGING EXPERIENCES!"*

One last thing I want to mention before you move on: don't worry if your friends and family think that your new Miracle expectations and guidance is crazy, because…

YOUR MIRACLE GUIDANCE IS NOT MEANT FOR THEM. IT IS MEANT FOR YOU AND YOU ALONE! Of course, they can't see it or believe it!

My intention is that by the time you're done reading this chapter, you can RELEASE FEAR on every level, which allows you to connect to your Miracle guidance, which guides you easily and effortlessly and then connects you to your Miracle world, where everything you ask for is manifested as your Miracle solution!

If you're finally ready to say, "Fuck you or forget you" to fear or any other obstacle that may be sidetracking you from your Miracle, move on to the FIRST STEP.

1ˢᵗ STEP: MIRACLE MINDSET

This section is not merely about positive thinking. This is MIRACLE MINDSET THINKING, to help you SHIFT YOUR THINKING INTO TRULY BELIEVING YOUR MIRACLES ARE POSSIBLE!

Know that your Miracle is already on its way. Why? Because being guided to this book and reading it was your REAL first step toward your NEW, MIRACLE-INFUSED life. Now, let's begin…

Miracle mindset thinking is all about the realization that nobody on Earth has a better answer about you and your life than you. You have your own MIRACLE GUIDANCE NAVIGATION SYSTEM that is waiting to guide you out of whatever hell-on-Earth situation you find yourself in. All YOU need to do is ASK so you can RECEIVE THIS GUIDANCE! This chapter is the place you come to when you're needing a Miracle solution, and nothing else will do!

This is when you decide to STEP BACK INTO YOUR POWER or, as I prefer to call it, YOUR SUPERPOWER. You stand up a little straighter, you pull your shoulders back and take a deep breath, then you say to yourself <u>or</u> out loud, to the OPPOSITION or THE WORLD…

> *"Fuck you, and your opinions. You have no INFLUENCE over me, my body, my family, or my life!"*

I realize saying that might feel a little harsh and crude; however, sometimes stepping into your power feels uncomfortable because you haven't done it for so long. Saying the above statement, even if it's just in my head, has helped me remember to not take everything the world dishes out. Instead, I can choose to say, "NO MORE!"

I now choose to NOT BELIEVE EVERYTHING that is said to me as if it's gospel, because it's often just somebody's opinion or an institutional belief with a cookie-cutter philosophy they've prepackaged for everybody. The thing is, I'm not "everybody," and NEITHER ARE YOU!

I had to come to this realization because of the many times in my life when the people I looked up to or the doctors I was seeking answers from said to me…

- I can't help you.
- I don't know what's wrong with you.
- I don't know why this medicine is not helping you.
- I don't know why your body is responding this way.
- I don't have any answers for you, and so on.

This is when I realized that all those people were NO BETTER than I was. Yes, they may have been specialists and experts in their field, but for years I had been treating them as if they were healers! More than healers, I was treating them as if they had some Divine connection to the answers I was seeking for my life, or – even worse – I was treating them as if they were some sort of God in my Universe! Ask yourself if you are doing that too. If so, that ends today!

True healers, just by their mere presence of EMANATING THEIR HEALING ESSENCE OF BELIEVING IN YOU and YOUR HEALING POSSIBILITIES, are a catalyst for your TRUE HEALING – mentally, physically, spiritually, financially, etc. True healers come from all walks of life, and often they don't even know they are healers; they're just at the right place at the right time to drop a PROFOUND BOMB OF INSIGHT AND GUIDANCE designed just for you… and then they move on!

This also means true healers don't even have to touch you, because their PURPOSE IS TO REMIND YOU…

"You are THE MIRACLE ALCHEMIST HEALER
in your life!"

Whether you believe this is through God, The Universe, or your Higher-self... it doesn't matter!

What matters is your resolve in deciding...

"FEAR DOESN'T LIVE HERE, ANYMORE!
THIS IS MY LIFE AND I CHOOSE A MIRACLE
EXISTENCE AND NOTHING ELSE WILL DO!"

It's time for you to start connecting and believing in your individual Miracle Guidance System, so LET'S BEGIN!

2nd STEP: RELEASING

This step is critical before you move onto the following steps because you need to RELEASE ANY BELIEF IN THE OPPOSITE OF THE MIRACLE YOU ARE ASKING FOR. Why? Because while YOUR HIGHER POWER AND/OR HIGHER SELF HAS UNLIMITED POSSIBLE MIRACLE SOLUTIONS, your belief (or lack thereof) can be blocking or slowing down their ability to intervene on your behalf.

Below, choose one or both AFFIRMATIONS to remind you that this situation is not your problem anymore. Then rewrite it below in the blank area until you have it memorized; this way you're confirming it to your conscious and unconscious mind.

- **I NOW choose to RELEASE…**

  Any FEAR that has EVER influenced my life, that I believed consciously or unconsciously, up to this moment!

- **From this moment forward, I LET GO…**

  Of all FEAR, worries or concerns that I have had about my life, and I NOW choose to create a NEW MIRACLE-LICIOUS REALITY!

Before you turn the page, repeat the following out loud…

"I NOW STEP INTO BEING THE MIRACLE ALCHEMIST
I came into this life to be!

AMEN, SO IT IS, THANK YOU!"

3rd STEP: CALL IN MIRACLE

This is a reminder that "WORDS TRULY ARE YOUR WAND," and when you speak you can CALL IN, COMMAND, CLAIM, BELIEVE, and use GRATITUDE to help create the Miracle future you want. Choose one or two MIRACLE MANTRAS below to repeat and think about often throughout every single day until your Miracle is here.

DOUBLE DOWN ON THIS whenever you are tempted to think and speak negatively or worry about anything that is opposite of the Miracle Solution you are wanting to manifest!

- **I NOW CALL IN…**

  My Miracle Angels of Deliverance from FEAR, as I trust and know I am guided only to Miracle solutions!

- **I NOW COMMAND…**

  That FEAR no longer has control over me, my life, my body, or my family! Only miracles surround us.

- **I NOW CLAIM…**

  That everyone in my household is surrounded and guided by Miracle energy. This energy neutralizes all FEAR in our mind, body, soul, and every area of our life, from this moment forward!

- **I NOW BELIEVE…**

  That ONLY MIRACLE SOLUTIONS are attracted to me, wherever I am and wherever I go!

- **I am NOW BLESSED…**

  That from this moment forward I step into my SUPERPOWER of being the FEARLESS Miracle Alchemist, Allower, and Receiver that I came here to be!

REPEAT the following out loud:

"THANK YOU, ALL POSITIVE UNIVERSAL ENERGY,
FOR HELPING ME CALL IN MY MIRACLES!"

4th STEP: ACTION ACCELERATOR

Intentional ACTIONS that guide you to Activate The Energy of Allowing to become a MIRACLE ALCHEMIST!

ACTION STEP:

ALLOW AT LEAST 5 TO 15 MINUTES the FIRST TIME you use this visualization; then only a minute or so, on and off throughout your day, when or if fear shows up.

1. Close your eyes and picture that moment FEAR about your situation showed up in your life!

2. Now, imagine seeing that situation on an old TV that has a VCR attached to it. You know, those ancient machines that use tapes and have "Rewind," "Play," and "Delete" buttons.

3. Push the rewind button and imagine that it's rewinding your memory to the beginning. Only this time, when you push play, you're going to imagine the Miracle situation that you wish would've happened.

Replay it repeatedly until you feel better. If the old memory keeps coming up, continue pushing the delete button and imagine pushing "re-record" on top of it. This works because you're now creating a new memory; the old memory starts to become unclear, and you will gradually release it more and more. If you want to take this a step further for faster results, read on.

IDEAS TO MAKE THIS MORE MAGICAL

Make this as fun as possible, as if it's something you would see at a circus or in a fairytale. I personally like to imagine I'm magical in my mind recording – that I can see and do things the other people who are part of this past "TV Mind Movie" cannot.

EXAMPLE:

I imagine I'm sitting on a unicorn with a magical rainbow in the background and angels and fairies are all around me, talking to me about how healthy or wealthy or loved and liked I am – basically, anything that makes me feel Miracle-licious. Then I have the people in my "TV Mind Movie" say Positive MIRACLE THINGS to me, like...

- "Bernadette, I forgot that you're a Miracle queen and everything always works out for you!"
- "Bernadette, you have the best Miracle ideas ever!"
- "Bernadette, I forgot you're like a Miracle unicorn, I'm so sorry I doubted you!"
- "Bernadette, I don't know what came over me and why I said that other stuff, because I really do believe in you and the Miracle life you are now creating!"

I use these fun and funny scenes in my head to replace what had really happened in a doctor's office, during a family disagreement, or anything I'm feeling in lack about. Keep in mind that sometimes these memories are just of me, and that's why I like to include the angels and fairies for a much-needed positive uplifting, Miracle energy that helps me not feel so alone! Remember, the more joy you can find and the more you can laugh, the easier it is to feel the old reality collapse and the new reality come to life.

This often helps me since I am surrounded by family members who are not spiritual; in fact, they are often very analytical and want scientific proof before they listen to me. I find talking to them very stifling, and they try to squash my Miracle ideas, and my hope! I talk in greater detail about this in my first book, *Believe It to Receive It: Activate the Miracles Waiting For You.*

These negative emotions are highly contagious, meaning they can easily spread from one person to another, infecting them and squashing their Miracles. Why? Because you CANNOT MANIFEST MIRACLES WITH THOSE NEGATIVE FEELINGS!

The TV movie memory is the antidote to that emotional contagion. It's the best way I have found to shift my energy and reprogram memories so they don't have negative control over me anymore – and it's fun!

Every time you choose to do this, it means you too are NOW CHOOSING TO SEE AND BELIEVE IN YOUR MIRACLE FUTURE!

DON'T FORGET:

Use all your senses – hearing, seeing, feeling, tasting, and smelling. The idea is to REALLY FEEL GOOD with this new TV movie, as this will help you release the old negative program of fear about your situation faster.

BONUS STEP

Here are some ideas on how to be more MIRACLE-LICIOUS and SEAL THE DEAL TO LOCK IN YOUR MIRACLE ALCHEMY!

LET'S PLAY THE MIRACLE GAME

Find a Miracle friend or relative who believes in Miracles. My aunt, who is eightyish now, is the biggest believer in me and supporter of my Miracles, ever! She's also good at playing "Let's pretend our Miracles are here now" on the fly. This means I can call her with no heads-up and say, "Let's talk about OUR MIRACLE LIFE, WEALTH, HEALTH THAT ARRIVES TODAY OR THIS WEEKEND, ETC."

Whenever I'm needing to solidify my Miracle a little bit more or I'm having a bad day instead of living in the Miracle world I want to live in, I call her. After talking for five minutes, we both believe in one another's Miracles a little bit more and the harshness of this world doesn't bother us so much!

Your goal for this game is to call someone who believes in Miracles. Tell them you've just had the MOST MIRACLE-LICIOUS, VISION, IDEA, OR WISH *EVER* about your Miracle_____ (fill in desire), and you wanted to share it with somebody who was positive and high vibe energy. Tell them you chose them because you knew they wouldn't give you any of that REALITY BS to tarnish your miracle vision.

Or

Tell them you found the best book ever that will help YOU BOTH MANIFEST YOUR MIRACLES FASTER – and that this book suggested this game and you want to play it with them because they're so high vibe and MIRACLE-LICIOUS. Remind them that this means they are delicious to Miracles too, so you knew they were the perfect teammate for this game!

The "Let's Pretend Our Miracles are Here NOW" game is simple and only takes five minutes. Each of you has a turn, and all you do during your turn is talk about and act as if the Miracle you want in your lives are CURRENTLY HERE NOW or WILL ARRIVE ON YOUR DOORSTEP ANY MINUTE!

Using the following prompts to guide you, talk in great detail about what YOUR MIRACLE VISION…

- looks like
- feels like
- smells like
- taste like, etc.

Include all the examples of things you know you will soon be able to have or do because your Miracle is coming true NOW, or at least ANY MINUTE, because you can just feel it, see it, and are believing in it more and more!

EXAMPLE: MIRACLE GAME PHONE CALL

PART 1:
I call a friend…RING, RING. She answers, "Hey, Bernadette, what's up?"

ME:
"I have a great idea. Let's talk about what it looks and feels like in our Miracle prosperous life as if it's happening NOW!"

FRIEND:
"Okay, you go first!"

ME:
"So I just had to call you and let you know that I was looking at my bank balance and realized MY MIRACLE finances that WE'VE BEEN TALKING ABOUT LATELY HAS JUST COME TRUE! Yes, I am

making money while I sleep! I have so many deposits into my account, I can't figure out where all this money is coming from – it is an actual Miracle! I called you today because I think the perfect way to celebrate this is for me to take us – you and me – on a Caribbean cruise!"

FRIEND:
"OMG, I am needing a cruise, I think this is THE BEST IDEA EVER!"

ME:
"Let's start investigating all our options and meet for lunch next week and talk about it – my treat!"

PART 2:
I then would actually schedule a real lunch date. It does not need to be fancy – it could even be at my house and we could look on the computer and find our perfect Caribbean cruise.

OF COURSE...
The other half of the conversation from Parts 1 and 2 would be about my friend's Miracle and what it looks like and how we're going to celebrate that too!

THEN:
FEARLESSLY keep living and breathing what your Miracle would look like (as you did in Part 2) as often as possible. Personally, anytime I am in a low-energy funk, and feel like my Miracle is too far away, I play this game by myself. I personally would continue investigating Caribbean cruises and choose which room I want and the best time of year to visit the different Caribbean islands, etc.

I'd even look up my deadline to put down a deposit to reserve my ideal room on the cruise. Because the more you can get excited and connect with the vision of your Miracle, the more high-vibe you are, which calls in your Miracle sooner!

I truly believe that talking to OTHERS WHO ARE POSITIVE AND BELIEVE IN MIRACLES ARE A CATALYST FOR YOUR MIRACLE ARRIVING SOONER, SO TALK ABOUT YOUR MIRACLE WORLD WITH ANYBODY WHO IS HIGH-VIBE ENOUGH TO HELP YOU BELIEVE IN IT, AS OFTEN AS YOU CAN. MOST IMPORTANTLY, HAVE FUN WHILE YOU'RE DOING IT!

Because you are saying out loud to The Universe…

> *"Here I am, I'll believe in you, and this is how I wish to see you…"* or *"Please show me an even BETTER MIRACLE-LICIOUS life than I can even imagine, ASAP.*
> *THANK YOU!"*

Miracle Goal

Miracle Magnet Placebos

"This Miracle begins when you decide that you're done with your present reality, and your ONLY answer is the illogical Miracle solution."

Unfortunately, I had to learn this when I had a multitude of problems with my health and doctors couldn't figure out what was wrong. One day, I suddenly realized that I had been treating doctors as if they were God and had all the answers I needed. This was unrealistic, expecting mere mortals to know my solution, when, obviously, my situation was outside the box of normalcy and needed a Miracle solution!

My healing came when I decided that The Universe had the answer to my Miracle and that I would be guided to it, even if I didn't know how, ONLY BECAUSE "I had asked for my Miracle solution to be revealed."

Healing came when I decided to step back into my power of owning my body and to stop giving away my healing power to doctors. After all, they were *not* the God of me!

This is when I learned the power of believing in MIRACLES or whatever I decided was my Miracle/placebo answer!

First, I want to clarify the definitions of "Miracle" and "Placebo" so there is no misunderstanding of the use of these terms in this chapter. Also, you may think this chapter is too farfetched, and I think the simplicity of these definitions makes them more believable and doable.

Definition Of Miracle
The New Oxford American Dictionary defines miracle as "A surprising and welcomed event that is not an explicable goal by natural or scientific laws and is therefore considered to be the work of divine agency."

Definition Of Placebo
"A harmless pill, medicine, or procedure prescribed more for the psychological benefits to the patient than for any physiological effect." ~New Oxford American Dictionary

YES... in this chapter, I am teaching you to ASK for guidance to your "PLACEBO," then DECIDE that this is your MIRACLE ANSWER, because ...

> *"Often for a Miracle to manifest all it takes is a decision that something, ANYTHING, is your Miracle solution.*
> *This decision creates a domino effect that bridges your Miracle from nothingness into existence!"*

Now, with this understanding, let's agree on the following:

- MIRACLES ARE NOT LOGICAL
- PLACEBOS ARE NOT COMPLETELY UNDERSTOOD
- MIRACLES ARE OFTEN UNEXPLAINABLE

And because of this, anyone who is wanting a Miracle should know…

"YOU WILL NEVER RECEIVE A MIRACLE IF YOU DO NOT FIRST BELIEVE IN IT!"

Now, flip the page as confirmation to The Universe that you are ready to begin the four steps of being a Miracle Alchemist!

1st STEP: MIRACLE MINDSET

This is not merely positive thinking. This is MIRACLE MINDSET THINKING to help you SHIFT YOUR THINKING INTO TRULY BELIEVING YOUR MIRACLES ARE POSSIBLE!

> *"Every day, trillions of Miracles happen around*
> *the world to somebody, somewhere.*
> *WHY NOT YOU, NEXT?"*

Know that your Higher Power and The Universe want to DELIVER MIRACLES to you, ASAP, by any means, people, places, and things. Make no mistake – there are infinite possibilities for Miracle solutions to your situation and the only limit is the limit you place on your Miracle.

You do this by believing in the lack of your Miracle, when you use your valuable energy to speak or think about the opposite of your Miracle situation.

From this moment forward, decide…

"I will only focus on what I want, and I will no longer breathe a word or think thoughts of poison, which is anything that is opposite of my Miracle life, which is now evident in every area of my mind, body, and affairs. The existence where my Miracle had not been evident yet, is no longer my reality.

I call fourth my Miracle Divine Destiny, where I am healthy in every area of my life and where my reality of_____ (fill in) IS NOW A DONE DEAL AND COMES TO PASS!

My Divine Destiny includes, but is NOT LIMITED to, my Higher Self's vision of my best intentions of health, wealth, love, and perfect self-expression of living my purpose in every area of my life. I will not except less because I am a MIRACLE ALCHEMIST!"

> **"YES… YOU ARE MAGICAL & MIRACLE-LICIOUS!"**

Now, let's begin your NEW MIRACLE STORY!

2nd STEP: RELEASING

This step is critical before you move onto the following steps because you need to RELEASE ANY BELIEF IN THE OPPOSITE OF THE MIRACLE YOU ARE ASKING FOR. Why? Because while YOUR HIGHER POWER AND/OR HIGHER SELF HAS UNLIMITED POSSIBLE MIRACLE SOLUTIONS, your belief (or lack thereof) can be blocking or slowing down their ability to intervene on your behalf.

Below, choose one or both AFFIRMATIONS to remind you that this situation is not your problem anymore. Then rewrite it below in the blank area until you have it memorized; this way you're confirming it to your conscious and unconscious mind.

- **I NOW choose to RELEASE…**

  The OLD reality of my situation; I no longer claim it as my truth!

- **From this moment forward, I LET GO…**

  Of thinking of myself as POWERLESS and that anyone else knows what is best for me more than I do!

Before you turn the page, repeat the following out loud:

"I NOW STEP INTO BEING THE MIRACLE ALCHEMIST
I came into this life to be!

AMEN, SO IT IS, THANK YOU!"

3ʳᵈ STEP: CALL IN MIRACLE

This is a reminder that "WORDS TRULY ARE YOUR WAND," and when you speak you can CALL IN, COMMAND, CLAIM, BELIEVE, and use GRATITUDE to help create the Miracle future you want. Choose one or two MIRACLE MANTRAS below to repeat and think about often throughout every single day until your Miracle is here.

DOUBLE DOWN ON THIS whenever you are tempted to think and speak negatively or worry about anything that is opposite of the Miracle Solution you are wanting to manifest!

- **I NOW CALL IN...**

  My Divine Destiny to NOW Manifest in every area of my life!

- **I NOW COMMAND...**

  The Universe to reveal my Miracle life that is full of INFINITE MIRACLE SOLUTIONS!

- **I NOW CLAIM...**

  That Miracle Angels are surrounding me to help guide me to my Miracle solutions with ease.

- **I NOW BELIEVE...**

  That Miracles surround me, every minute of every moment of every day, guiding me to MY MIRACLE LIFE & DIVINE DESTINY.

- **I am NOW FILLED WITH APPRECIATION...**

  That I am now guided easily and effortlessly to my Divine Destiny full of infinite Miracle solutions.

REPEAT the following out loud...

"THANK YOU, ALL POSITIVE UNIVERSAL ENERGY, FOR HELPING ME CALL IN MY MIRACLES!"

4th STEP: ACTION ACCELERATOR

Intentional ACTIONS that guide you to Activate The Energy of Allowing to become a MIRACLE ALCHEMIST!

Decide right NOW, at this moment, to BELIEVE that EVERY IDEA you receive is MIRACLE GUIDANCE to Your Miracle Answer. Thus, every idea becomes YOUR PLACEBO MIRACLE ANSWER!

This means you are believing that your Higher Power and/or The Universe and all Miracle energy is guiding you! Everything that is guided to you is a SOLUTION, thus activating your Miracle.

You are now on high awareness, believing you are guided through seeing, hearing, feeling, and a knowingness that Miracle solutions surround you. Believe that no matter how the answer shows up, you will recognize it. Then you will follow through with whatever guidance is given to you, even if it seems outrageous!

This means you are consciously looking and expecting Miracle solutions at every place you visit and from every person you speak to. Everything you see or hear holds the possibility of giving you Miracle guidance to your Miracle Divine Solution.

Once you realize that you can decide what is your Miracle answer is, you will become more confident in The Universes and YOUR HIGHER SELF's ability to communicate to you.

Examples of what this looks like:

- One time I was guided to read a magazine, and in that magazine was information on exactly what my rare condition was. I then knew what to ask my doctor to do to help with it, because most doctors have not been trained or are familiar with that condition.

  (The full story is in my course, "Miracle Accelerator: Fast Track Your Miracles for Unlimited Manifestations.")

- Another time, after two years of trying medication to help my severe depression and anxiety and getting no relief, I decided that the next prescription I was given, no matter what it was, would be my placebo answer! (The full story is in the introduction of my book, *Believe It To Receive It: Activate The Miracles Waiting for You.*)

These are just two examples, but it gives you an idea of how you can be **guided to OR decide** what your placebo answer is. Some people, after hearing those stories, instantly know what their placebo answer is. However, even if they don't relate exactly to your situation, don't worry, because just having the belief that you have your Miracle answer creates the energy that brings the ACTUAL Miracle to you sooner – like it did for me with the prescription. I remember literally saying to my doctor, "Whatever you give me today is MY ANSWER, because I'm ready to get on with my life."

Now, if you are NOT somebody who instantly knows what you can label as your Miracle Placebo answer, no worries, because I have created the following action steps to help guide you to a "PLACEBO DIVINELY GUIDED ANSWER JUST FOR YOU!"

PART 1: ACTION STEP

Say out loud and fill in below information. Remember to plug into your Inner Guidance.

ASK…
"Divine Miracle Energy of The Universe and/or Miracle angels, please surround me now and give me CRYSTAL-CLEAR MIRACLE GUIDANCE TO MY MIRACLE SOLUTION for_____
(Fill in your situation) by this date or sooner_____. (Fill in a date at least seven days away.)

> *"My new reality is, I believe, I ASK, and it is given.*
> *I have asked, so this means*
> *IT IS GIVEN!*
> *My Miracle solution, NOW COME TO LIGHT AND*
> *MANIFESTS!"*

NOTE:
This time limit is NOT BECAUSE THE UNIVERSE NEEDS IT.

It is for YOU to STAY MORE FOCUSED and ALERT AT THIS TIME!

PART 2: ACTION STEP

ALLOW AT LEAST 5 TO 15 MINUTES.

Find a blank page in the journal section at the back of this book and journal the following:

1. Each night before bed, review your day and write down…

    *   Any guidance that comes to you and do not judge it as being silly or illogical.

    *   Notice the power of three. (This is anything that comes to you three times or more because The Universe repeats messages and three times normally gets your attention.)

    *   Anything that seems like a synchronistic opportunity to hear something or see something just "by chance."

2. At the end of seven days, review ALL JOURNAL ENTRIES using your Inner Guidance to reveal YOUR PLACEBO MIRACLE ANSWER. This can be guided to you through a good feeling about a particular topic or a knowing what your next step should be; or, once you've read all the entries it seems obvious, almost as if it jumps off the page.

    NOTE:

    If definite guidance does not seem to come to you instantly, don't worry. Before you fall asleep, ask for your Higher Power and/or Higher Self to reveal to you, "BY THE END OF TOMORROW NIGHT," exactly what your Next Best Step should be.

3. **Important Placebo TRICK**

    If you still feel insecure and don't know what answer you should choose as your Placebo Miracle, JUST DECIDE ON ONE IDEA. Oftentimes, this GOOD FAITH STEP forward activates your Miracle solution to reveal itself to you. Why? Because this relaxed energy (when you're not worrying) is a catalyst for your Miracle!

Now, with this peace of mind, realize that you cannot go wrong. Miracles often come to you just by virtue of your decision that "I AM READY FOR MY MIRACLE AND NOTHING ELSE WILL DO!"

BONUS STEP

Here are some ideas on how to be more MIRACLE-LICIOUS and SEAL THE DEAL TO LOCK IN YOUR MIRACLE ALCHEMY!

Confirm out loud that your Miracle solution is here now. This means when anybody asks, "What's new?" or "How are you?" you're going to answer with a MIRACLE **SELF-FULFILLING PROPHECY**, such as:

- "I'm doing better than ever, because I know the Miracle I've been asking for is on its way!"
- "I'm pretty sure my Miracle solution has been activated; I can feel it coming!"
- "I'm so glad you asked, because I believe my Miracle prayer has been answered!"

If people then ask, "Tell me more," "Please share," or "Tell me every detail," just say to them...

- "I am guided to not reveal any details until the Miracle is complete."
- "I'll tell you more next time I see you because I have to get to my next appointment."
- "Thank you for asking, but I'm a firm believer of not rushing Divine timing by sharing details until the Divine deal is done... We will talk soon!"

I have found leaving conversations on THIS POSITIVE NOTE ACTUALLY HELPS CALL MY MIRACLE TO ME SOONER.

PLUS, MY FRIENDS AND FAMILY ARE THEN SAYING TO ONE ANOTHER, "DID YOU HEAR THE GOOD NEWS OF BERNA-DETTE'S MIRACLE SOLUTION?" AND THIS HIGH-VIBE ENERGY OF BELIEVING IN ME ACTUALLY HELPS EMPOWER ME TO COMPLETE MY MIRACLE FASTER!

Unbeknownst to them, they are helping me!

Miracle Goal

More Miracles of Love

When I was a hairstylist, people would often tell me in detail their hope for love, romance, or more love in their current relationships. I was always so amazed how often people focused only on their appearance – changing their hair color and style, or – the biggest change almost everyone wanted to make – losing weight. Because they just "knew" if they made at least one of those changes, they would find true love or their current mate would fall hopelessly back in love with them again.

And I would say to them...

"Tell me all the different ways that you show yourself that you love you."

After I said this, there would always be an awkward silence, as if I had just said something obscene or spoke in a different language. Then they would concentrate, trying to figure out the answer to this question. In fact, this quietness of their deep thoughts would create a heaviness in the room that made the atmosphere very uncomfortable for both of us!

So, let me be so bold as to ask you, the reader, who's reading this right now...

What are three ways you show love to yourself? As you think about this, I want you to think about whether this self-love is obvious to other people in your life...

This means if we were to ask your mate or best friend to tell us three ways you show love to yourself, they would easily know the answer to this question, because you unapologetically love yourself and it's evident to anybody who pays attention to you.

Was that a hard question for you to answer, or was it easy?

I had to really think about that one, because it made me feel selfish or righteous, as if self-love is something to be ashamed about.

Now I have another question, and I promise it's easier to answer. Give me three examples of ways you would love to be loved by someone else. This can be a romantic, platonic, or family type of love.

Were you able to answer this question a whole lot faster than the previous question?

Most people I speak to are able to answer that question without much thought.

I believe that is because we know what kind of love we want from others; in fact, most often...

- It's the kind of love that is lacking in your current life
- Was missing in your life as a child
- Absent in your last relationship, etc.

The previous questions were intended to make you think about all the different ways you are living and breathing self-love in every area of your life. Why? Because I truly believe that we are the ones who teach the world the acceptable behaviors for showing LOVE to us.

This is also an example of the Law of Attraction, that "like attracts like." We will only attract to ourselves people who treat us like we treat ourselves, or how we believe we should be treated.

I've always believed…

> *"That you must first love thyself to be able to*
> *unconditionally love others.*
> *AND for you to allow others to truly Love you."*

I say this statement knowing that it is not easy for some people to hear. Due to numerous life circumstances and situations that they had no control of, they may lack trust in others, self-love, and/or have unrealistic expectations of love.

However, please stick with me as I give you a funny personal story that will help clarify this point even more.

First, let me set the stage…

My husband and I had some friends over for dinner. I don't remember who or how many, but I'll never forget this conversation because I never saw it coming!

At this time, we had been married for about twenty years and I had NEVER HEARD any sort of statement like the following come out of my husband's mouth, ever!

(Please note, I'm paraphrasing this conversation to the best of my ability.)

Suddenly I heard my husband respond to somebody's comment with the following words…

"I knew when we were first dating that Bernadette was high maintenance, and that if I was going to get and keep her I would need to be able to afford her!"

Hearing this come from my husband made me gasp with horror, because I'd never considered myself "high maintenance," "money hungry," or in need of a "sugar daddy!"

So, I said to him …

"What are you talking about? I met you when neither one of us had money, I've never expected you to take care of me, or that you would provide for me!"

He then said …

"Bernadette, I'm not blind. I saw that you get your hair and nails done all the time, massages regularly, and other self-indulgent items. Just look in your closet!"

I then laughed and said …

"Honey, I was in the beauty industry as a hairstylist when we first met. I never had to pay for any of that. I would just trade other people my services for their services!"

He looked at me with utter and complete surprise, and we had a good laugh about it!

However, I must admit that he was correct to a certain extent. Once you become accustomed to lavishly taking care of yourself, you come to expect it, so I've continued most of those monthly (and sometimes weekly) services to this day.

I tell you this funny story because it was a light bulb moment for me. For the first time ever, I realized that those self-care experiences were just one small example of how I love myself, and how it could be interpreted by others, positively or negatively, depending on their own ability to gauge self-love.

Since self-love is the foundation for giving and receiving more love, let's begin with the following simple definition. The rest of this chapter will be about how to incorporate the love vibration into your life as a Miracle magnet!

According to the Miriam Webster Dictionary, SELF-LOVE is "Proper regard for and attention to one's own happiness or well-being."

Now that we are on the same page about self-love, let's talk about how to IMPROVE YOUR SELF-LOVE and how this is a magnet for health and love. This way, you can start attracting the MIRACLE OF LOVE that you want and deserve in all areas of your life.

1ˢᵗ STEP: MIRACLE MINDSET

This is not merely positive thinking. This is MIRACLE MINDSET THINKING to help you SHIFT YOUR THINKING INTO TRULY BELIEVING YOUR MIRACLES ARE POSSIBLE!

Today is the day that you can choose to alchemize your life into the Miracle-licious, loving life you have always wanted. By continuing to read this chapter and taking the following steps, you are now beginning the alchemical process that will help you RECEIVE MORE LOVE and GIVE MORE LOVE than you ever thought possible!

Yes, it is possible with this one intention to change your whole life, to feel more love and be more loving. I'll never forget the day this profound truth changed my life forever.

It was the day after my husband had a heart attack at only thirty-three years old. At the time we had been married for ten years, and for the last two years we had been talking about divorce because we had fallen out of love with each other (honestly, we were not loving ourselves either.) Though I wanted to save the marriage, I no longer recognized my husband or myself and was wondering if it was a lost cause.

As soon as I walked into my husband's hospital room, this is what he said to me…

"Bernadette, I have decided to love you again, and I will treat you the way I treated you when we were in love in the very beginning of our relationship."

Hearing this was a dream come true! I'm not going to lie and say that instantly we were like teenagers in love again; however, I will say that in that moment I felt more hope and love than I had felt in the last few years of our relationship. It was a Miracle, hearing my husband say that he INTENDED TO LOVE ME AGAIN AND WORK ON OUR MARRIAGE.

NOTE that he did not say, "What are you going to do for me?" or "I expect the same from you." What he did say was so unemotional and very matter of fact and not how I fantasized or I wished he would've said it! But I understood and believed his INTENTIONS, and I knew without a doubt we would love one another again… and we did. We've been together for over THIRTY YEARS!

What my husband didn't know is the secret ingredient I'm going to share with you. Every time during those difficult two years, whenever I thought of him I would send him love. When I was angry at him, I would send him the INTENTION OF LOVE and ask the angels to magnify this energy to be more loving toward him.

I then would imagine he was surrounded with a beautiful pink light of love and angels. I did this because I knew being MORE LOVING, UNCONDITIONALLY, could heal our marriage!

Since I didn't always feel true love for him, I did the next best thing I could do, which was send him intentions of love with no expectation of receiving anything back. Surprisingly, it made me feel better; it helped my heart not hurt so much from the fear and feeling of our marriage dying.

This is when I learned…

> *"HOW POWERFUL INTENTIONS ARE when you mix it*
> *with THE INTENTION OF LOVE… IT'S HEALING!"*

I truly believe LOVE HEALED OUR MARRIAGE and WITHOUT A DOUBT I KNOW LOVE HEALED HIS HEART TOO!

(The full story is in Chapter 5 of *Believe It To Receive It: Activate The Miracles Waiting for You.*)

Next, let's begin with releasing the situation so the Miracle Alchemy of LOVE can begin!

2ⁿᵈ STEP: RELEASING

This step is critical before you move onto the following steps because you need to RELEASE ANY BELIEF IN THE OPPOSITE OF THE MIRACLE YOU ARE ASKING FOR. Why? Because while YOUR HIGHER POWER AND/OR HIGHER SELF HAS UNLIMITED POSSIBLE MIRACLE SOLUTIONS, your belief (or lack thereof) can be blocking or slowing down their ability to intervene on your behalf.

Below, choose one or both AFFIRMATIONS to remind you that this situation is not your problem anymore. Then rewrite it below in the blank area until you have it memorized; this way you're confirming it to your conscious and unconscious mind.

NOTE:
In this chapter you are releasing unforgiveness because it is the opposite of Love. If forgiveness is a challenging word for you, you could use the words "INTENTION for FORGIVENESS."

- **I NOW choose to RELEASE...**

  And forgive everyone in my life, including myself, who has NOT loved me unconditionally (100%).

- **From this moment forward, I LET GO...**

  Of all past feelings and beliefs from any time in my life when I did not feel loved by others, or I withheld love from others. I intend for this to create a healing for all souls involved in this situation _____. (Fill in.)

Before you turn the page repeat the following out loud…

"I NOW STEP INTO BEING THE MIRACLE ALCHEMIST
I came into this life to be!

AMEN, SO IT IS, THANK YOU!"

3rd STEP: CALL IN MIRACLE

This is a reminder that "WORDS TRULY ARE YOUR WAND," and when you speak you can CALL IN, COMMAND, CLAIM, BELIEVE, and use GRATITUDE to help create the Miracle future you want. Choose one or two MIRACLE MANTRAS below to repeat and think about often throughout every single day until your Miracle is here.

DOUBLE DOWN ON THIS whenever you are tempted to think and speak negatively or worry about anything that is opposite of the Miracle Solution you are wanting to manifest!

- **I NOW CALL IN...**

  Angels of Love, and I ask them to help me love myself unconditionally so that I can completely heal from the inside out.

- **I NOW COMMAND...**

  The Love of The Universe to surround me in every nook and cranny of my life with 100% pure, unconditional Love so that I can know and feel I am worthy of Love in every area of my life.

- **I NOW CLAIM...**

  That I love my body and appreciate everything it does for me, and that every Miracle bodily process I took for granted is now loved, blessed, and healed.

- **I NOW BELIEVE...**

  That the healing power of Love surrounds my mind, body, and soul, so that from this moment forward every area in my life is now healed and restored to my highest loving possibilities for this lifetime.

- **I am NOW FILLED WITH APPRECIATION...**

  Because I know, without a doubt, the Love of The Universe surrounds me and all its inhabitants with only 100% pure Love. I now absorb this Love, and I am healed from the inside out. Because I know as we heal individually, we heal the world one person at a time.

REPEAT the following out loud ...

"THANK YOU, ALL POSITIVE UNIVERSAL ENERGY,
FOR HELPING ME CALL IN MY MIRACLES!"

4th STEP: ACTION ACCELERATOR

Intentional ACTIONS that guide you to Activate The Energy of Allowing to become a MIRACLE ALCHEMIST!

ACTION STEP:

ALLOW AT LEAST 15 MINUTES & DO THIS AS MUCH AS POSSIBLE DURING THE WEEK.

This is where you're going to combine action and words to begin the ACTIVATION OF LOVE. This begins with the action of you LOVING YOURSELF UNCONDITIONALLY or, at the very least, acknowledging your body and the Miracles that it provides for you daily!

Next time you take a shower, bath, or put on lotion, massage it into your body from your head to your toes, talk to your body and tell it you love it.

Touch each part of your body, especially the parts you are not happy with and would like to be healthier or more in shape, etc. **Because Love is fundamental to health and healing, Miracles CAN BEGIN WITH THE INTENTION TO LOVE IT…. even before you do!**

This LOVING ACTION will be one of the things that will help you to accelerate your body's healing process or, if you're ALREADY healthy, this process will help you too emanate the steady vibrational energy of Love, which will help you attract even more MIRACLE LOVING circumstances in your life.

FACE EXAMPLE:
While Putting lotion on your face daily, say…

- "I love my beautiful face and all its unique qualities."
- "I am so blessed to have eyes that allow me to see my loved ones."

- "I'm so grateful for my nose because it gives character to my face. As I breathe in air to my lungs it also filters this air to be healthier to nourish my body."
- "I'm so thankful to have ears so that I can hear the world around me, and I can hear my loved ones."
- "I am so blessed to have these lips and mouth, because it allows me to smile to express the joy from my heart."

NOTE:
If you have a part of your body that is not working properly, disfigured or in anyway, imperfect to you, say the following:

I love you _____. (Fill in body part.) Even though you're not perfect, I appreciate you and I know you're healing now.

Or

_____ (Fill in body part), today I decided to start loving you and thank you for the lessons you have brought into my life about being more unconditionally loving or forgiving, etc. Thank you.

Or

_____ (Fill in body part), I'm sorry that I have been angry at you and neglected you. Today I have decided to start loving you and I intend to love you into Miracle healthiness and healing. Thank you for cooperating!

REMEMBER
Once you do this regularly, you will be amazed how much those parts of your body that are not ideal don't bother you anymore. Then, gradually, your body will unconsciously start morphing into your ideal body; sometimes, without much work, or other times, you will become more motivated to start working out or eating healthier, all because you decided to appreciate and intend to love your body. WHEN WE LOVE OURSELVES, IT RADIATES FROM OUR BODY AND ACT AS A MIRACLE MAGNET, ATTRACTING MORE LOVE FROM THE UNIVERSE!

BONUS STEP

Here are some ideas on how to be more MIRACLE-LICIOUS and SEAL THE DEAL TO LOCK IN YOUR MIRACLE ALCHEMY!

Here are my favorite little MIRACLE-LICIOUS tricks to get your glow on:

Have you ever noticed that there's some people who seem to glow from the inside out? It's as if they have this aura of light coming from them and surrounding them. Did you know this is easy to do?

1. Plug in to your Higher Power and/or Higher Self, then take a deep breath and see and feel this guiding diamond light connecting you to from your heart center up toward the heavens and down toward Mother Earth. Imagine this beautiful radiant light is filled with love from The Universe, to you and from you, as you are now connected to The Universe. Then feel this radiant light emanating from the pores of your skin out into The Universe.

2. Take some deep breaths of this beautiful, loving energy and light until you can you feel this Love pulsating and emanating from you.

NEXT
Affirm all day long, no matter what you're doing or who are you with and even if you're alone, "I love you, I bless you, and I send you Love."

Imagine this is just a frequency you are sending to the world today. Then imagine blowing out this unconditional Love from your heart center, everywhere you go, to whomever you see today, and whatever you do.

If at any time during the day you become tired or irritable, this means you lost your connection to the Source energy. Just close your eyes and plug in to this loving light again!

Don't be surprised when people start to notice something about you that's different but can't seem to put their finger on it. You will know it's because you have this loving glow that radiates from the inside out and this vibration of Love becomes a Miracle magnet for Miracle circumstances that seem to follow you wherever you go.

Miracle Goal

Receiving Miracle Money
In Desperate Times

I think it's important to share with you the exact frame of mind I had when I first learned HOW TO MANIFEST MIRACLE MONEY during the most desperate time of my life!

This way, you will never feel that your situation is too much or impossible. Please know that this information is giving you a glimpse of my heart and soul, so please be gentle with your comments. Sharing this is ONLY for the purpose of helping you, and regrettably, I must think about the time of my life when I wanted to disappear!

I'm hoping this transparency will help give you a clear idea of the zero-option thinking I was in, because it will give you framework of the laser-focus MIRACLE THINKING you can choose to step into when you are wanting to manifest MIRACLE MONEY too.

At the time, my husband and I had been married for a year and our son was about eight months old. I was still having severe, postpartum depression and anxiety. I was seeing a psychiatrist that specialized in depression, with little relief. To make matters worse, we'd just received a letter of eviction from our house and had thirty days to vacate. Also, we received a letter of repossession of a piece of equipment my husband used for work because of lack of payment. On top of all this, the renter who was renting our previous house was a few months behind on rent; and since there was no sign of him buying it like he had promised, my husband and I were about to lose that house too.

I want you, the reader, to know that I purposely used the word "disappear" because I didn't think of it as killing myself. I thought of it as ending the pain. It was never about life or death for me; it was about ending the pain of life because I didn't feel alive; I felt dead inside already. I believed my existence was adding more stress to our situation than helping.

I don't like talking about the worst times of my life, because I truly believe that "thoughts become things" and "words are our wand," so NOW I truly ONLY think and talk about things I want to be true currently, and in the future.

However, I know there are a lot of people who could benefit from learning more about the MIRACLE MONEY I helped manifest during the worst time of my life, especially since I didn't leave the house 99% of the time. Please keep in mind that I wasn't the only ingredient in this story, and we'll get to that a little bit later, but I think it's important to know that we didn't receive the money because we worked our asses off! I wasn't in a space emotionally to leave the house and my husband did everything he could do, including working fifteen or more hours a day, and still that was not going to pay our bills!

I just want to clarify that because I'm sure there's somebody here who needs to hear this...

"It's NOT the hustle that brings in your MIRACLE MONEY, it's the ability to LET GO of the HOW your MIRACLE MONEY will arrive. It's believing there is an answer to your situation that is bigger than you, and anything you can possibly ever imagine."

As far as I'm concerned, HUSTLING is the OPPOSITE of ALLOW-ING; in fact, it can BLOCK YOUR MIRACLE MONEY!

Next, we will begin understanding what ALLOWING TO RECEIVE MIRACLE MONEY looks like.

1ˢᵗ STEP: MIRACLE MINDSET

This is not merely positive thinking. This is MIRACLE MINDSET THINKING to help you SHIFT YOUR THINKING INTO TRULY BELIEVING YOUR MIRACLES ARE POSSIBLE!

> *"MIRACLE MONEY thinking is pure focus on*
> ***ONLY WHAT YOU WANT,***
> ***NOT the HOW!***
> *Literally, you are giving NO ENERGY or OXYGEN*
> *to anything opposite of your Miracle!"*

This is going to get a little sticky, especially if you're not a "God" believer. I give two examples below, but I will refer to one just for simplicity, so please bear this in mind because most likely your ego is going to get a little triggered in about one minute!

Just hang in there and try to accept the concept that YOUR LIFE IS ABOUT TO CHANGE, MIRACULOUSLY, because this information is the FOUNDATION TO YOU BEING A MIRACLE ALCHEMIST!

First, when I am manifesting MIRACLE MONEY, the following MIRA-CLE MANTRA is what I align myself with because it instantly gets me into THE MIRACLE MINDSET that I need to be in. It is…

> *"GOD IS MY SOURCE AND MY SUPPLY."*
> *Or, if you prefer…*
> *"THE UNIVERSE IS MY SOURCE AND MY SUPPLY."*

This is from my favorite teacher, Florence Scovel-Shinn, who was a metaphysician one hundred years ago… or, I could say, SHE WAS "A MIRACLE ALCHEMIST!"

To help yourself get aligned with believing in MIRACLE MONEY, say the above mantra repeatedly like a broken record, any time you are feeling stressed or overwhelmed or worried, to reprogram your thinking and believing into allowing!

This Miracle Mantra seems so simple, yet most people don't understand the depth of it. When you are saying, "God is my source and my supply," that means GOD IS MY SUPPLY OF EVERYTHING, including ALL THE DIFFERENT AVENUES that money is delivered to me.

It's a reminder that your source of money or income is…

- NOT the child support you receive monthly
- NOT the IRS who owes you money
- NOT your job with the weekly deposits
- NOT the money owed to you from varies places
- NOT the alimony that's due to you
- NOT your family member who always loans you money

It's a reminder to not give the power away to a false God, your ego, or your human self. It is also a reminder that these other avenues are not the original source!

Whoop, are you still with me?

I know that's a hard concept for a lot of people to accept…unless you have desperate circumstances, like I did, when I didn't have a job and my husband was working himself to exhaustion and we were on the verge of losing everything!

And, just in case you're wondering, we did end up having a happily-ever-after MIRACLE MONEY story. Because one day when my husband was at work doing concrete at somebody's house, they asked him if he wanted to buy a raffle ticket for their child's school. My husband said yes, and we won $10,000, which saved us from losing everything; and the renter DID end up buying our other house within those thirty days. Notice my hubby did not go looking for a raffle or any other way to win money. The Miracle money came to him.

If you want more details about *exactly* what I did to help energetically for our MIRACLE MONEY, with more examples of how I incorporated that thinking from the Miracle Mantra into my everyday life (even though I didn't leave the house), and the tools that help me overcome that depression, check out *Believe It To Receive It: Activate The Miracles Waiting For You.* I truly believe my husband and I helped with that Miracle in different ways, yet, MIRACULOUSLY neither of us had any idea what the other was doing.

In summary, this MIRACLE MINDSET MANTRA allows you to release ownership of the problem with just a few words, and helps you to remember that it's not your job to figure out how the MIRACLE MONEY will come to you. It's your job to...

> *BELIEVE IN YOUR SOURCE OF SUPPLY AND ASK TO BE GUIDED... IF THERE'S ANY STEPS FOR YOU TO DO TO HELP WITH THIS MIRACLE MONEY, THEN TRUST YOU WILL BE GUIDED... THEN ALLOW!*

Next, we need to begin releasing this situation so that the Miracle Alchemy of Money can begin!

2ⁿᵈ STEP: RELEASING

This step is critical before you move onto the following steps because you need to RELEASE ANY BELIEF IN THE OPPOSITE OF THE MIRACLE YOU ARE ASKING FOR. Why? Because while YOUR HIGHER POWER AND/OR HIGHER SELF HAS UNLIMITED POSSIBLE MIRACLE SOLUTIONS, your belief (or lack thereof) can be blocking or slowing down their ability to intervene on your behalf.

Below, choose one or both AFFIRMATIONS to remind you that this situation is not your problem anymore. Then rewrite it below in the blank area until you have it memorized; this way you're confirming it to your conscious and unconscious mind.

- **I now choose to RELEASE…**

  The idea that I need to figure out HOW my MIRACLE MONEY arrives. I now accept that "God is my source and my supply!"

- **From this moment forward, I LET GO…**

  Of thinking of myself as small or unimportant in this Universe! Because I came into this life to play BIG, and this includes abundance in every area of my life!

Before you turn the page repeat the following out loud ...

"I NOW STEP INTO BEING THE MIRACLE ALCHEMIST
I came into this life to be!

AMEN, SO IT IS, THANK YOU!"

3rd STEP: CALL IN MIRACLE

This is a reminder that "WORDS TRULY ARE YOUR WAND," and when you speak you can CALL IN, COMMAND, CLAIM, BELIEVE, and use GRATITUDE to help create the Miracle future you want. Choose one or two MIRACLE MANTRAS below to repeat and think about often throughout every single day until your Miracle is here.

DOUBLE DOWN ON THIS whenever you are tempted to think and speak negatively or worry about anything that is opposite of the Miracle Solution you are wanting to manifest!

- **I NOW CALL IN…**

  The infinite MIRACLE MONEY of The Universe to surround me and everyone I love!

- **I NOW COMMAND…**

  The wealth of The Universe to answer my every wish and desire. I believe that ASK AND IT IS GIVEN. I am asking, knowing I shall receive!

- **I NOW CLAIM…**

  Divine abundance to surround me, in every area of my life, as it showers the abundant Love of The Universe on me with more wealth than I could ever imagine!

- **I NOW BELIEVE…**

  _____ (Fill in your source) is my source and my supply!

- **I AM SO GRATEFUL FOR…**

  The divine blessing of MIRACLE MONEY that arrives in my life unexpectedly by the end of this week!

REPEAT the following out loud…

"THANK YOU, ALL POSITIVE UNIVERSAL ENERGY,
FOR HELPING ME CALL IN MY MIRACLES!"

4th STEP: ACTION ACCELERATOR

Intentional ACTIONS that guide you to Activate The Energy of Allowing to become a MIRACLE ALCHEMIST!

ACTION STEP:

Allow at least one minute every morning for the following accelerating steps until your Miracle money has arrived!

THE HAPPY DANCE

This my favorite ACTION for money manifestations, but it could be used for any Miracle you want.

This step is all about showing that you are believing in your MIRACLE MONEY *before* it arrives. I created this because every day I visualize that the Miracle (of anything) I want has ALREADY ARRIVED, and this has become my symbolic HAPPY DANCE to pre-celebrate my Miracle. Of course, I also do this dance when my Miracle arrives; wherever I am and whatever I'm doing, I stop and do this dance, because it helps lock in my energy field. This dance means MY MIRACLE HAS MANIFESTED – plus, I truly feel MIRACLE-LICIOUS while dancing!

HOW TO CREATE A HAPPY DANCE

- Think of fun, outrageous 2-to-5 little movement or steps you do with your legs and arms to celebrate receiving your MIRACLE MONEY.

- BONUS POINTS if you can make this as silly and funny as possible. Remember, fun, happy energy accelerates your Miracles!

- Then start doing this dance, no matter what, every morning when you get out of bed in CELEBRATION and PRE-BELIEVING that your MIRACLE MONEY finds you today!

OPTION 2: FOR ANYONE WHO IS NOT PHYSICALLY ABLE TO DANCE:

- Create a short song – it can be only a few words long – that is joyful and funny to sing about your Money Miracle arriving today!

  Or

- Create in your mind a happy dance and imagine yourself doing it while singing a celebration song or prayer about the arrival of your MIRACLE MONEY today!

REMEMBER

Your mind is extremely powerful, and it's been scientifically proven that your body believes everything your mind tells it. (I talk more about this in Chapter 3 of *Believe It To Receive It: Activate The Miracle Waiting For You.*)

So, even if you can't dance and sing physically right now, imagine that you can… and what better way to do this than receiving money at the same time!

ALSO:

If you want to see my happy dance, it is on my website, Themiracleologist.com

BONUS STEP

Here are some ideas on how to be more MIRACLE-LICIOUS and SEAL THE DEAL TO LOCK IN YOUR MIRACLE ALCHEMY!

DO TIIIS FOR 5 MINUTES, EVERY DAY

RIP THIS PAGE OUT AND HANG ON YOUR MIRROR.

Stand in front of the mirror and, while you're looking into your eyes, speak to the depths of YOUR SOUL & HIGHER POWER as you say out loud…

1. I BELIEVE God is my source and my supply. Repeat 3 times.
   (Above, fill in with our Higher Power.)

2. I NOW ASK for my MIRACLE MONEY from The Universe to find me.

3. I NOW TRUST with my whole heart and soul that if there is anything The Universe needs me to do to help with for this Divine alignment of my MIRACLE MONEY, I WILL RECEIVE CRYSTAL CLEAR GUIDANCE easily and effortlessly.

4. I NOW ALLOW for at least this AMOUNT OF MIRACLE MONEY OR MORE_____. (fill in)

5. I AM NOW SO THANKFUL THAT BY THIS DATE _____ (FILL IN) I WILL RECEIVE MY MIRACLE MONEY FROM GOD AND MY DIVINE UNIVERSE!
   (Above, fill in your Higher Power.)

6. THANK YOU, THANK YOU, THANK YOU!

Miracle Goal

The Secret Ingredient To Being A Miracle Alchemist

$\mathcal{I}$ remember the first time this hit home for me. I was out shopping in a grocery store, which is one of my least favorite things to do, and suddenly remembered my favorite aunt/second mom telling me, *"Bernadette, just be grateful you have money to buy food for your family."* So I said a little prayer of gratefulness for money and food to feed my family.

However, I also was absolutely miserable because at that time I had idiopathic hives (idiopathic means the doctors couldn't figure out why I had them), and they covered my legs and were atrociously uncomfortable! While feeling sorry for myself, I suddenly noticed a man who had shorts on in the middle of winter and his legs were just covered with sores and scabs. I thought to myself, *"Hmmm… I bet there are people who don't have legs, and they possibly would wish to trade us for our imperfect legs!"* I then realized I could be thankful for what I have, even with its imperfections.

From that moment forward, I began to do gratitude mantras and prayers, especially when I was most uncomfortable from the hives. This meant off and on throughout my whole day, I preoccupied myself with gratitude, instead of the misery of my body.

The solution for the hives was not instant, but I noticed that concentrating on being grateful gave me some relief from the itching as my mind was preoccupied with something besides my misery and problems.

However, the answer soon came for my Miracle solution, and I truly believe, without a doubt, that being grateful daily for what I did have, and not concentrating on what I did not have, helped raise my vibration to allow me to attract and receive the Miracle solution I was needing for that issue. When I was guided to the cause of the issue and to the healing, I knew, from that moment forward, that I WAS A MIRACLE ALCHEMIST. Honestly before the healing even came, I knew I was healed!

Next let's talk about how to make transmuting your problems into Miracle solutions easy and fun!

1ˢᵗ STEP: MIRACLE MINDSET

This is not merely positive thinking. This is MIRACLE MINDSET THINKING to help you SHIFT YOUR THINKING INTO TRULY BELIEVING YOUR MIRACLES ARE POSSIBLE!

REMEMBER, AS YOU BECOME A REAL, LIVE MIRACLE ALCHE-MIST, you are making the decision that from this moment forward you will love and appreciate where you are currently, whatever that looks like. If this is difficult then, at the very least, find things to be thankful for in your life currently. Also, as a Miracle Alchemist you no longer give time, energy, or thoughts to negative things in your life; this includes the negative things around you in the world, news, or circumstances with your friends and family. Because focusing on any negativity is taking away from the positive energy needed to allow your Miracle to be guided to you.

YES, APPRECIATING WHAT YOU HAVE begins to accumulate positive energy that surrounds you, and this positive energy acts as a Miracle magnet. On the other hand, when you are fearful, afraid, worried, or any other negative feeling, the positive energy begins to deplete, instead of accumulating in your energy field to act as YOUR MIRACLE MAGNET.

In this chapter, you will learn how to truly believe and become thankful BEFORE the Miracle solution you're asking for ACTUALLY APPEARS!

**Next, you will learn how to release any
UNAPPRECIATIVENESS!**

2nd STEP: RELEASING

This step is critical before you move onto the following steps because you need to RELEASE ANY BELIEF IN THE OPPOSITE OF THE MIRACLE YOU ARE ASKING FOR. Why? Because while YOUR HIGHER POWER AND/OR HIGHER SELF HAS UNLIMITED POSSIBLE MIRACLE SOLUTIONS, your belief (or lack thereof) can be blocking or slowing down their ability to intervene on your behalf.

Below, choose one or both AFFIRMATIONS to remind you that this situation is not your problem anymore. Then rewrite it below in the blank area until you have it memorized; this way you're confirming it to your conscious and unconscious mind.

- **I now choose to RELEASE...**

  Unappreciativeness, unhappiness, unhealthiness, unworthiness, and any LACK thinking, or the illusion that I am not enough, or I don't have enough... in all areas of my life.

- **From this moment forward, I LET GO...**

  Of the following situation_____ (fill in) and any obsessive negative thoughts that believe I cannot have exactly the Miracle I am asking for.

Before you turn the page repeat the following out loud...

"I NOW STEP INTO BEING THE MIRACLE ALCHEMIST
I came into this life to be!

AMEN, SO IT IS, THANK YOU!"

3rd STEP: CALL IN MIRACLE

This is a reminder that "WORDS TRULY ARE YOUR WAND," and when you speak you can CALL IN, COMMAND, CLAIM, BELIEVE, and use GRATITUDE to help create the Miracle future you want. Choose one or two MIRACLE MANTRAS below to repeat and think about often throughout every single day until your Miracle is here.

DOUBLE DOWN ON THIS whenever you are tempted to think and speak negatively or worry about anything that is opposite of the Miracle Solution you are wanting to manifest!

NOTE:

This is the ONLY CHAPTER that gives examples of various ways to use ONLY GRATITUDE AS YOUR WAND to help you manifest the Miracle future you want.

- **I am NOW THANKFUL...**

  That the Miracle solution to my situation has been answered easily and effortlessly.

- **I am NOW GRATEFUL...**

  For all the expected and unexpected Miracles NOW appearing in every area of my life.

- **I am NOW FILLED WITH APPRECIATION...**

  That my every MIRACLE WISH and DESIRE is NOW fulfilled with Miracle ease and grace, in Divine and perfect ways!

- **I NOW AM SO BLESSED...**

  To believe WITHOUT A DOUBT that the Miracle solution I am seeking is easily revealed and guided to me in Divine ideal timing.

REPEAT the following out loud...

*"THANK YOU, ALL POSITIVE UNIVERSAL ENERGY,
FOR HELPING ME CALL IN MY MIRACLES!"*

4th STEP: ACTION ACCELERATOR

Intentional ACTIONS that guide you to Activate The Energy of Allowing to become a MIRACLE ALCHEMIST!

NOTE:

The following Action Step has strict guidelines. This is because, in the beginning, it will take an extraordinary amount of focus to notice your Miracle language communicating the guidance to you. That said, please know this Action Step is a favorite of mine because of its powerful results!

ACTION STEP

ALLOW AT LEAST 5 TO 15 MINUTES.

Take a walk outside alone, with no distractions or obligations to anybody else, BECAUSE YOU'RE WORTH IT! This means turning your phone off, no music or other people (including children, if you're able). This is your time for ONLY YOU to fill your heart with Love and Gratitude as you listen to the quiet voice of your soul talking to you, through The Universe that surrounds you, about your life.

1. Plug in and imagine reconnecting to your Higher Power and/or Higher Self on a soul level.

2. REPEAT: "With every step that I take, I release through the bottom of my feet all negativity or energy that is opposite of the Miracle energy that I want and deserve in every area of my life. I am so thankful to Mother Earth for transmuting this energy into love, light, and Miracles!"

3. NOW, as you walk, look up at the SKY/HEAVEN… see the clouds, the sun, or the moon. Find as many things as possible to be thankful for! Then, with each item, repeat, "I am so thankful for this beautiful_____." (fill in.)

4. Then, look at the things that surround you on MOTHER EARTH. Find anything to be thankful for on the landscape you're walking on – the trees, the flowers, a beautiful building, the community that surrounds you, the technology, or other things that help make our life so much easier. As you find as many items as possible to be thankful for, repeat to yourself, "I am so thankful for _____." (fill in.)

5. NOW, IN THIS ELEVATED HIGHER VIBRATION ENERGY, THINK OF YOUR PARTICULAR MIRACLE WISH and ASK FOR MIRACLE GUIDANCE TO THE

NEXT BEST STEP TOWARD YOUR MIRACLE. Allow whatever thought comes to you with no judgment, and if you need clarification just ask for it.

6. THEN BE GRATEFUL THAT THE MIRACLE SOLUTION YOU ARE SEEKING IS NOW GUIDED TO YOU EASILY AND EFFORTLESSLY. Even if you have not received any tangible guidance yet, ACT AS IF YOU HAVE!

7. As you return to your original destination, imagine RECEIVING YOUR MIRACLE WITHIN THE NEXT 24 HOURS. See this and feel it with your whole heart and soul; imagine what it would taste like, smell like, and how it would feel in your hands. Imagine every detail of your Miracle as if it IS NOW FULFILLED and, as you imagine this, be THANKFUL EVEN MORE!

BONUS STEP

Here are some ideas on how to be more MIRACLE-LICIOUS and SEAL THE DEAL TO LOCK IN YOUR MIRACLE ALCHEMY!

Be aware that what I'm about to suggest is harder than it seems. I know, because I have spent decades working on this idea and still occasionally catch myself doing the opposite.

TRY TO NOT COMPLAIN ABOUT ANYTHING, AS LONG AS YOU POSSIBLY CAN!

- For one hour
- One day
- One week

The hidden gem of this bonus step is that you will suddenly realize how often you and the other people around you are also complaining. Seeing the positivity or the negativity of those you choose to surround yourself with, and how their attitudes and emotions can be contagious, will help you make the adjustments (i.e., limiting the time you spend with certain people) necessary to keep your vibe high.

Remember, the energy that surrounds you, acts like a radio wave that pulsates like a magnet to The Universe. It can bring you MORE THINGS TO BE THANKFUL FOR OR MORE THINGS TO COMPLAIN ABOUT. Either way, "your thoughts become things and your words are your wand" and you are creating your reality!

Miracle Goal

Raising Your Vibe & Becoming Unstuck

*"If you always do what you've always done,
you'll always get what you've always got."*

~ Henry Ford

I believe that the bored, stuck feeling comes only when it's time to move on to new ideas, scenery, or a new stage in life. In other words, this feeling is really your soul talking to you, telling you it's time to expand and try new things… or it's a sign that you're going in the wrong direction, and you need to rethink what your ideal Miracle Life looks like.

I've already shared with you a little bit of the following, but it's worth repeating since it's easy to forget… AND SO LIFE-CHANGING IF YOU CAN PAY ATTENTION TO IT!

Here is an example of what it feels like when you're raising your vibe and becoming unstuck:

I have noticed that when I receive guidance for my Next Best Step toward my Miracle life, and IF I TAKE THAT FIRST STEP (even if

I'm a little nervous because sometimes change can be uncomfortable), then soon, magically, I can feel my energy shift to a higher vibration, which makes it easier to trust and follow the next step. Why? Because this internal guidance is LIFTING MY BODY and SOUL UP, from the inside out, WITH THIS ALMOST ELECTRIC, GOOD FEELING that confirms I'm on the right path. Then another step will show up for me to take, and then another and another step until – BOOM! – MY MIRACLE ARRIVES!

The trick is to remember that NOTHING MORE will show up until I take that first step of this Miracle guidance. Also, this Miracle guidance often seems to have nothing to do with my Miracle, or it will seem like a ridiculous idea or inspiration. But, because I've listened to this Miracle guidance so often, I now recognize it when it appears and I easily trust and follow it without worry.

However, when I'm going in the wrong direction or any direction that is not ideal and Miracle-licious, then I will feel stuck, stagnant, and blocked from the good I've been asking for.

During times like this, I become stressed, depressed, feeling hopeless, and just blah, and it's all because I asked for more and did not follow through on my part: taking the NEXT STEP I was guided to, which allows The Universe to align me with this ideal Miracle situation for my Miracle solution!

Here's a great analogy for this human tendency: imagine you were in your car and entered an address in your Google maps for a destination you're wanting to go to. Then, as soon as the first direction shows up on the console, you put your car in park and stare at the screen, waiting for your destination to appear. You have not moved from your original location, so the GPS has not been activated to tell you what to do next.

In the meantime, you are wondering whether the map is turned on, did it lose connection, or did it forget your request. You then decide, "I'm not doing anything until, I get a definite next step; I want proof Google can take me to where I want to go." In other words, I WANT TO SEE IT FIRST, BEFORE I BELIEVE IT!

So, out of fear, you don't go anywhere. Before you know it, your car runs out of gas and you become hot and miserable sitting in one spot waiting, doing nothing. Then you decide to go inside your house because at least there you're comfortable. Except for the fact that you know you are supposed to be somewhere else, and this makes you feel utterly miserable, depressed, stuck, lost, and losing hope of ever getting to your destination.

All the while, you're secretly believing the Google God and the whole Universe has let you down, because shouldn't everything come to you, INSTANTLY, with NO REAL ACTION on your own behalf?

The answer is NO! I've never seen it work that way… unless it's a Divine Intervention Miracle, for example, saving a life when it was not time for that person to die.

However, this chapter is about how to raise your vibe to call in the Miracle energy that surrounds you. This helps you become unstuck so the next time you receive guidance, you will recognize it and take the first step towards the Miracle life you have been asking for, instead of waiting hopelessly, doing nothing, and then feeling lost and alone, like your Higher Power or The Universe has forgotten you.

Because I truly believe that,

"ASK, AND YOU SHALL RECEIVE!"

Now that you've made it this far, don't close the book and stop yourself from receiving MIRACLE GUIDANCE. Keep reading and, once and for all, let's break the cycle of ASKING FOR YOUR MIRACLE BUT NOT FOLLOWING THIS GUIDANCE.

1ˢᵗ STEP: MIRACLE MINDSET

This is not merely positive thinking. This is MIRACLE MINDSET THINKING to help you SHIFT YOUR THINKING INTO TRULY BELIEVING YOUR MIRACLES ARE POSSIBLE!

REPEAT AFTER ME ...

"I am now ready to welcome the new and release the old. I am now allowing my mind, body, and soul to receive an upgrade energetically in every area of my life, to the highest vibration that I can handle, and with this I call forth my highest path and purpose for this lifetime. I NOW Step into my new and improved Miracle-licious life. _____.
(Fill in your name.)

I WILL NO LONGER ...

- *Be stagnant in my life, feeling like it's going nowhere.*
- *Having just enough or barely getting by.*
- *Settling for anything that is less than my best possible outcome for my current situation.*

I AM NOW ASKING FOR ...

CRYSTAL- CLEAR GUIDANCE TO THE "NEXT BEST STEP" OF MY MIRACLE LIFE!

I NOW DECLARE ...

I CONFIDENTLY FOLLOW ALL GUIDANCE THAT IS GIVEN TO ME, BECAUSE I AM A MIRACLE ALCHEMIST! THAT IS JUST WHO I AM!

Take a deep breath, acknowledge this declaration and the new Miracle energy that is surrounding you. Take another deep breath, then move onto the next step when you feel READY to RELEASE feeling ENERGETICALLY STUCK.

2nd STEP: RELEASING

This step is critical before you move onto the following steps because you need to RELEASE ANY BELIEF IN THE OPPOSITE OF THE MIRACLE YOU ARE ASKING FOR. Why? Because while YOUR HIGHER POWER AND/OR HIGHER SELF HAS UNLIMITED POSSIBLE MIRACLE SOLUTIONS, your belief (or lack thereof) can be blocking or slowing down their ability to intervene on your behalf.

Below, choose one or both AFFIRMATIONS to remind you that this situation is not your problem anymore. Then rewrite it below in the blank area until you have it memorized; this way you're confirming it to your conscious and unconscious mind.

- **I NOW choose to RELEASE…**

    The old energy in my life to welcome the new. I allow The Universe to transmute this old stagnant energy into new Miracle Alchemy energy that surrounds every area of my life.

- **From this moment forward, I LET GO…**

    Of anything in my mind, body or soul, or any other area of my life that is holding me back from stepping into this NEW, IMPROVED MIRACLE VERSION OF MYSELF THAT I NOW CALL FORTH!

Before you turn the page repeat the following out loud…

"I NOW STEP INTO BEING THE MIRACLE ALCHEMIST
I came into this life to be!

AMEN, SO IT IS, THANK YOU!"

3rd STEP: CALL IN MIRACLE

This is a reminder that "WORDS TRULY ARE YOUR WAND," and when you speak you can CALL IN, COMMAND, CLAIM, BELIEVE, and use GRATITUDE to help create the Miracle future you want. Choose one or two MIRACLE MANTRAS below to repeat and think about often throughout every single day until your Miracle is here.

DOUBLE DOWN ON THIS whenever you are tempted to think and speak negatively or worry about anything that is opposite of the Miracle Solution you are wanting to manifest!

- **I NOW CALL IN…**

  Miracle angels to surround me with positive energy, guiding me to my ideal Miracle life!

- **I NOW COMMAND…**

  The Universe to have positive energy full of Miracles that surrounds me in every area of my life, lifting me up to my highest path and purpose for this lifetime!

- **I NOW CLAIM…**

  That I am NOW on a Miracle path of positivity. Wherever I go and whomever I am with experiences the rippling effect of this positive energy that is now a flowing current of Miraculous opportunities in my life!

- **I NOW BELIEVE…**

  That I AM A MIRACLE ALCHEMIST, and any stuck or stagnant energy I now transmute into vibrant positive energy of opportunities, for every area of my life!

- **I AM SO GRATEFUL…**

  For the positive changes NOW flowing into every corner of my life, attracting Miracle after Miracle with the highest intentions of Miracle possibilities.

REPEAT the following out loud...

*"THANK YOU, ALL POSITIVE UNIVERSAL ENERGY,
FOR HELPING ME CALL IN MY MIRACLES!"*

4ᵗʰ STEP: ACTION ACCELERATOR

Intentional ACTIONS that guide you to Activate The Energy of Allowing to become a MIRACLE ALCHEMIST!

ACTION STEP

ALLOW AT LEAST 30 MINUTES, EVERY DAY FOR A WEEK.

During times of feeling stuck it is crucial that you move energy physically so you can start receiving the energy of Miracle guidance.

This physical movement is really for you to start calling in and activating the Miracle energy that ALWAYS SURROUNDS YOU but may feel currently stuck; or, this feeling is an actual reflection of being stuck mentally or physically in a current life situation.

Take an honest look at the following areas in your life for their energetic symbolic correlation.

- BEDROOM = Romance and love life.
- KITCHEN = Healthiness in your life.
- FAMILY ROOM = Your family life.
- OFFICE SPACE = Business/financial, abundance in your life.
- AUTOMOBILE = Where you are going in life.

Yes, I am saying that these areas with signs of neglect, clutter, piles of papers, dust, or cobwebs could be a visual example of the energetic clog in your life that is feeling so stifling.

Pay special attention to those areas, because …

> *"What your world looks like around you in your home, office or even your car, can be a visual example of what is ACTUALLY going on in your life and energetically in your world."*

This ACTION STEP is the belief that thoughts and ideas are also energy, even though we cannot see them. Therefore, when you're feeling stuck in any area of your life, what you really need to do is receive some new Miracle energy of ideas that can move you toward your Miracle goal or get you going in a new direction.

The quickest way to get Miracle energy moving in your direction is to, again, physically, move energy around you. Essentially, this ACTION STEP is all about you moving and clearing at least one or more of the above suggested areas. This can be reorganizing and cleaning items, either through dusting or wiping them off and, when appropriate, washing or giving items away that no longer serve your intended higher vibration. You might also consider moving stuff around, mixing it up, or putting it in different rooms, because this action is also moving the energy that surrounds you to help get energy moving in your life again!

Don't worry; this may seem like a lot to do, but for the purposes of this exercise you're only focusing on one area (of course, do more if you feel motivated). Also, this ACTION will feel good, almost like you can feel the stuck energy that surrounds you moving. **EXPECT MIRACLE GUIDANCE and MIRACLE ANSWERS TO BE REVEALED IMMEDIATELY WHILE DOING THIS STEP! I always receive my best Miracle ideas during this time of clearing, and so will you.**

Also remember that doing this ACTION STEP for as little as 30 minutes a day we'll start getting Miracle energy moving in your life again without overwhelming you. So, stop what you're doing right now and go find a room to begin clearing energy in, because…

This will help CREATE A CLEARER PATH FOR MIRACLE ENERGY TO FIND YOU. Remember, this stagnant energy that surrounds you COULD BE THE ONLY THING STANDING BETWEEN YOU AND YOUR MIRACLE LIFE!

NOTE:

If cleaning or releasing items are not easy for you to do, repeat the following Miracle Mantra while clearing.

> *"I NOW release the old me to welcome the NEW ME. I easily and effortlessly make room in every area of my life for New, Improved Miracle items and experiences of the highest value, vibration, and intention to easily find me."*

ALSO:

If you want more guidance and information to make this process even easier, I wrote a whole chapter on it in *Believe It To Receive It, Activate The Miracles Waiting For You.*

BONUS STEP

Here are some ideas on how to be more MIRACLE-LICIOUS and SEAL THE DEAL TO LOCK IN YOUR MIRACLE ALCHEMY!

Do something NEW POSITIVE AND DRAMATIC in your life, for example...

- Move to a different location.
- Start a new job.
- Cut or change your hairstyle, beard, or mustache.
- Take a vacation, even if it's just a long drive on a weekend, because the new environment will feed your soul and give you NEW IDEAS!

Be aware that big items like this often create instant Miracle changes, so this step is only for the true Miracle Alchemists, who are ready for their New Miracle life!

Miracle Goal

Your Life Purpose or a More Purposeful Life

$\mathcal{D}$id you notice that I didn't say FIND your life purpose? This is because I don't believe it's lost.

I believe we are taught to be too limited in thinking about our life purpose. In fact, I wonder if more people said, *"I want to find more purpose in my life"* there would be less stress and they would actually be able to understand their life purpose more easily!

The topic of life purpose is so daunting and has an assumed finality that I take issue with. In other words, I don't believe that we find our life purpose, do it for a little while, and then, before we know it, we've completed our life purpose and it's time for our life to be over.

I believe your life purpose is never-ending and keeps EVOLVING! I know with each passing year I find more purpose in my life, and I find different aspects of myself that I can enjoy as I utilize these positive aspects; this then creates more meaning in my life. Because as I focus more on the positivity of who I am, the other aspects or things that I wish were not true about me start to gradually fade away. As I give less energy to those things I do not want to be true in my life anymore, the positive things about me expand and I find more and more purpose and positivity – career opportunities, more income, Divine timing, family harmony, and kismet events, etc.

Now, let's talk about what a life purpose is, because it can have many different labels and interpretations. The other term I will refer to, passion, is in the way Oprah Winfrey explains it:

> *"Your true passion should feel like breathing,*
> *It's that natural."*

I remember watching an episode of *The Oprah Winfrey Show* when she talked about how to turn your passion into your career. This following statement was life-changing for me.

> *"You know it's right because you would do it for nothing*
> *and find a way to be able just to do it, in order to be able*
> *to continue. That's how you know you're doing what you're*
> *supposed to be doing."*

As a reference point for this chapter, I created the following explanation, which is my interpretation of what PASSION & PURPOSE may look or feel like:

Most likely it is something you've done almost your whole life, but you may have called it a hobby or something you've done for fun, often to escape reality. You find it energizing; this does not mean you don't occasionally get tired while doing this PASSIONATE PURPOSE, but more often than not it invigorates you and gives you an extra breath of fresh air to help you keep going. You may or may not notice that others are mesmerized by you when you're in your zone of doing this passion, because you make it look easy and others may find it difficult. It may or may not create income for you – do it anyway because it adds more purpose to your life.

Start today embodying the idea that…

> *"You were born with a PASSION that helps you get up every day and gives YOUR LIFE MORE PURPOSE! This is nothing new for you, and it is not lost or truly forgotten. It just is a part of who you are, like the color of your eyes or that funny noise you make when you laugh. It is just you, and it's so much you that you don't think about it and may have misplaced it. Now it's time to call it forth AGAIN and bring a PASSIONATE LIFE FULL OF PURPOSE BACK INTO YOUR REALITY!"*

Let's end this segment with a little story of how your life purposes can be revealed to you in bits and pieces throughout your life without you even knowing it. This should help shed light on your own situation and hopefully expand your ideas of your own more PURPOSEFUL LIFE!

When I was in elementary school, it was very hard for me – especially this one day when I flunked a test. In frustration, I said to my dad, *"My best friend is good in math and the teacher said one day she's going to use math in a job for something important… but Dad, I'm not good with anything in school. What will I be and do?"* Without missing a beat, my dad said something to me that changed my life forever, because for the first time I was told something about myself I had never known.

He said…

> *"Bernadette, you're a people person and you're really good with talking to people and not everybody is good at that!"*

At this time in my life, my dad had no idea I would graduate from high school with a cosmetology degree then use this ability to pay my way through college and get an Associate of Arts degree.

Even now, my dad and I reminisce about that time of my life. He recently said, *"I didn't know how you would make it through school, it was so hard for you."* I replied, "Well, thank goodness I was good at talking, because it gave me the edge and ability to talk to my teachers and ask for extra help. It all balanced out!"

The interesting thing is that now that I'm an author, I have people say they love reading my books because it feels like I'm speaking personally to them. Little do they know that I am – literally! I created these books using voice dictation because I'm not good at typing. This was easy for me to accept because I knew I was good at talking. All I had to do was figure out the best computers for voice dictation and everything else just fell into place.

I don't let the vastness of the things I'm not good at control my life. I just keep doing and improving the things I am good at, and this has brought more opportunities in my life such as being called an author and Miracle Expert.

But if you were to ask me, what my life purpose is, I would say…

I'M A LIGHT WORKER.

"I give hope to the hopeless by shining light on life's dark issues, because I believe that if I can make it out of the "hell on earth" I had found myself LOST in, YOU CAN TOO!

I write books and send them with love, out into the world, as beacons of light, to inspire others to climb out of the depths of their darkness too, so that they will shine their passion and purpose in this world and together we will light it up, one person at a time."

As you read this chapter, keep an open mind that your job title or career goal may only be a vehicle for you to apply your PASSION for a more PURPOSEFUL LIFE and your TRUE LIFE PURPOSE may be something that's incredibly difficult, like being a GOOD PARENT or a KIND GROCERY STORE CLERK, because – and now I'm going to quote my dear old dad – *"Not everybody is good at that!"* So obviously being a GOOD and KIND person is truly something we need more of, and it may take a Miracle for more people to realize that their TRUE LIFE PURPOSE is something as simple as being GOOD & KIND while shining their radiant smile, at us everyday people who, after a long day at work, walk through their line at the grocery store!

Now that you have a grasp of the endless possibilities for a PURPOSEFUL, PASSIONATE LIFE, let's see what new ideas you can come up with!

1st STEP: MIRACLE MINDSET

This is not merely positive thinking. This is MIRACLE MINDSET THINKING to help you SHIFT YOUR THINKING INTO TRULY BELIEVING YOUR MIRACLES ARE POSSIBLE!

> *"You were created with a purpose to do something that nobody else can do, exactly the way you do it!"*

There is a reason that you wake up every morning, and because you keep waking up every morning you have proof of a life purpose that is not fully completed – or it has evolved and you're stepping up into a more expanded version of yourself.

From this moment forward, decide that you will no longer settle for mediocre because you came here to be a MIRACLE MANIFESTING ALCHEMIST! You will no longer say, *"I don't know what my life purpose is."*

Instead, from this moment forward, you are going to say...

> *"I know without a doubt that I have a DIVINE DESTINY, and I BELIEVE that IF I ASK IT IS GIVEN, so I NOW ASK the Miracle Energy that surrounds me for DIVINE INTERVENTION to guide me to my more PURPOSEFUL life, and in a way that I will understand, easily and effortlessly, this DIVINE PLAN that I came into the body to accomplish for this lifetime, and I TRUST IT IS NOW REVEALED TO ME!*
>
> *Thank you!"*

Now you will begin this self-discovery by releasing ownership of this situation so the Miracle of Alchemy CAN REVEAL a MORE PURPOSEFUL LIFE!

2nd STEP: RELEASING

This step is critical before you move onto the following steps because you need to RELEASE ANY BELIEF IN THE OPPOSITE OF THE MIRACLE YOU ARE ASKING FOR. Why? Because while YOUR HIGHER POWER AND/OR HIGHER SELF HAS UNLIMITED POSSIBLE MIRACLE SOLUTIONS, your belief (or lack thereof) can be blocking or slowing down their ability to intervene on your behalf.

Below, choose one or both AFFIRMATIONS to remind you that this situation is not your problem anymore. Then rewrite it below in the blank area until you have it memorized; this way you're confirming it to your conscious and unconscious mind.

- **I NOW choose to RELEASE…**

  Any beliefs that I need to be more perfect, angelic, and better than who I am currently, to know and completely understand the depths of my life purpose!

- **From this moment forward, "I LET GO…**

  Of any mental blocks to knowing or understanding my highest path and purpose for this lifetime.

Before you turn the page repeat the following out loud…

"I NOW STEP INTO BEING THE MIRACLE ALCHEMIST
I came into this life to be!

AMEN, SO IT IS, THANK YOU!"

3rd STEP: CALL IN MIRACLE

This is a reminder that "WORDS TRULY ARE YOUR WAND," and when you speak you can CALL IN, COMMAND, CLAIM, BELIEVE, and use GRATITUDE to help create the Miracle future you want. Choose one or two MIRACLE MANTRAS below to repeat and think about often throughout every single day until your Miracle is here.

DOUBLE DOWN ON THIS whenever you are tempted to think and speak negatively or worry about anything that is opposite of the Miracle Solution you are wanting to manifest!

- **I NOW CALL IN...**

  My Higher Power, angels, and guides to reveal to me my exact "LIFE PURPOSE."

- **I NOW COMMAND...**

  Heaven and Earth to surround me with a beautiful, white guiding light that reveals to me MY HIGHEST PATH AND PURPOSE FOR THIS LIFETIME.

- **I NOW CLAIM...**

  To know exactly what my LIFE PURPOSE is, and I now fulfill it with ease and grace, because I am Divinely guided.

- **I NOW BELIEVE...**

  That I am Divinely guided, with crystal-clear understanding of the exact DIVINE DESTINY I came here to fulfill and that nobody else can fulfill but me!

- **I AM SO BLESSED...**

  To be guided easily and effortlessly to my LIFE PURPOSE with a crystal-clear understanding of my Next Best Step to being the MIRACLE ALCHEMIST I came here to be.

REPEAT the following out loud...

*"THANK YOU, ALL POSITIVE UNIVERSAL ENERGY,
FOR HELPING ME CALL IN MY MIRACLES!"*

4th STEP: ACTION ACCELERATOR

Intentional ACTIONS that guide you to Activate The Energy of Allowing to become a MIRACLE ALCHEMIST!

ACTION STEP

ALLOW AT LEAST 20 MINUTES FOR THIS.

Find a blank page in the journal section at the back of this book. As you go through the following visualization exercise, you will be prompted to answer some questions that will help guide you to your purpose and passion. NOTE: For each question there are some ideas in case you get stuck.

1. **Say out loud:**

   "MIRACLE ENERGY," I ASK for your guidance as I NOW choose to have fun, reviewing and realizing my life purpose, and I claim to easily see, hear, feel, know and understand, any messages that come through …for me… about having a PURPOSE-FUL LIFE.

   AMEN, SO IT IS, THANK YOU!"

2. **Close your eyes and imagine that you are a child about 8 to 10 years old, and you just had a bad day. What would you typically do to help yourself feel better?**

   - Did you talk to somebody?
   - Did you read a good book?
   - Did you write things down?
   - Did you play or do an activity?

3. **Now, think about a good day when you were about 12 to 15 years old. What did you do to have fun?**

   - Possibly a sport or hobby.
   - Something with a group or individually.

- Maybe you did this thing when you were supposed to be doing homework.
- Maybe you enjoyed it so much you decided to start making money by doing it.

4. **Now, imagine your childhood through your teenage years, possibly even college. What is something people complimented you on and/or something you found so easy it didn't even feel like work? So easy you wondered why people complimented you on it?**

   - This could be a school subject.
   - It could be something you were obligated to do but, again, didn't feel like work (i.e., a school activity, or a chore.)
   - Was there anything that you won awards for?
   - Did others or teachers compliment you on a particular ability, often in your life and you never thought it was such a big deal?

5. **If you didn't need money to survive, what would you do daily to pass time?**

6. **What is a passion of yours that you wish you could make money while doing?**

7. **When you were a child, what did you imagine you would grow up to do or be?**

8. **Is there anything you wish you would've gotten a degree or certification in?**

9. **Why did you choose to do your current career or job?**

10. **Write down any positive aspects you can think about a current or past job.**

11. **Ask family and friends what they always thought you would or should do as your life purpose, career, side hustle or for fun.**

REVIEW YOUR ANSWERS:

Look at the big picture of your life. Look for synchronistic opportunities that were given to you, common themes, and even general ideas that keep flashing in your mind. Write it all down, sensor and judge nothing. Sometimes all The Universe needs is for you to see it on paper and hold it in your hands. Then it wakes up your soul and reminds you who you really are.

BECAUSE A MORE PURPOSEFUL LIFE IS REALLY ABOUT BEING TRUE TO YOURSELF and has nothing to do with obligations, education, or money. Because when you are living your PURPOSEFUL LIFE, the money will show up as needed, especially as you get more crystal clear with who you are… ON A SOUL LEVEL!

To help with this process. I'm going to give you an example of how it all comes together when you stay open-minded with childlike wonder, NOT ADULT LOGIC! When I first did this process, I realized that all my answers to the questions above revolved around me writing, teaching, and helping people. However, originally I only thought of teaching to children in a school setting, and that idea brought me anxiety, not joy.

Then I began to journal all the possible ways I could teach, but not to children. I also began to wonder what I could teach about, because my ego began to speak up, only with negativity and I heard things like, "You don't even know how to type, you haven't picked up a computer in ten years, what possibly could you teach other people about? You weren't even good in school!"

Then I thought about my career as a hairstylist. I remembered the only time I really enjoyed being at work was when I was helping people be more positive about their situation.

I then asked my Higher Power for guidance. I pull oracle cards daily, and I kept noticing that a particular card about books kept showing up. This card meaning was, "Your life purpose involves books." At that time of my life, I had never considered writing a book. All I knew for sure was I wrote almost daily in my journal as therapy to unwind and gather my thoughts. But this idea of writing a book lit my soul up, and I felt more alive than I had felt in a long time every time I considered it.

Since just the idea of writing made me feel so happy, I knew that this was my Inner Guidance telling me I was on the right track. Even though I did not know what I would write about, I committed myself to writing at a certain time every day. I wrote with dedication for three months before I realized what my book was supposed to be about, and that was when my first book came alive and Bernadette, the author, was born. I truly felt like I had been *reborn.*

Remember…

> *"Your ego will show you all the reasons you shouldn't or couldn't have a more PURPOSEFUL LIFE, but your higher power will show you all the reasons that none of that stuff matters. All you need to do is take that first step toward the direction you are being guided to and then trust the path will light up and guide you, one step at a time, out of your mediocre life into a more, 'PURPOSEFUL LIFE!'"*

BONUS STEP

Here are some ideas on how to be more MIRACLE-LICIOUS and SEAL THE DEAL TO LOCK IN YOUR MIRACLE ALCHEMY!

From this moment forward you're going to "walk the walk and talk the talk" of a person who is on a higher path and purpose for this lifetime!

This means that your life purpose will be revealed to you more and more, especially now after reading this chapter. You're going to act as if it's already been revealed to you. Because believing and showing faith in something you can't see YET helps it to show up even faster in your life. Why? BECAUSE YOU'RE LIVING AS IF IT'S ALREADY TRUE!

This BONUS STEP is asking you to start making choices from your Higher Self's point of view in your day-to-day activities, as if you are already the person who is living their life purpose.

Here are some examples of things to ask yourself daily:

- Is this something my Higher Self would choose?
- Is this choice coming from a person who believes in Miracles or a person believing in fear?
- Is this choice the best decision for all parties involved?
- Am I making this decision from a place of fear or from a place of love?
- Is my Higher Self giving me guidance, or am I listening to my logical ego self?

Remember, as you begin to step into your life purpose you will be vibrating at a higher frequency that is guiding you on your highest path of possibilities for this lifetime.

So, if you find that certain people, places or things do not agree with you anymore, know this is no problem because…

> *"You will need to release the old in order to welcome the new…to make room for the ideal people, places, and things WHO ARE ALSO IN MORE ALIGNMENT WITH WHERE YOU'RE GOING, INSTEAD OF WHERE YOU'VE BEEN!"*

In Closing

I truly believe endings are only new beginnings, and every day is a fresh start to believe in your MIRACLE-LICIOUS LIFE MORE. For extra help, here's an acronym for a SECRET CODE FOR ALCHEMISTS:

A - Allowing Miracles Is Easy When There Is No Fear

L - Love Is A Secret Power When It's Unconditional

C - Catalyzing Miracles Begins In Your Mind

H – Heal Thyself, First and Always

E - Elixirs Are Made From The Energy Around You

M - Miracles And Manifestation Are Your Divine Right

I - Imagining Is Your First Step To Transmuting

S - Shift Energy By Changing Your Focus

T - Transform Only When You're Guided

And don't forget … NEVER ACCEPT DOOM as an acceptable answer to your challenge, because there's a Miracle solution for every situation!

My promise is that I will keep believing in you and your MIRACLE-LICIOUS life coming true! Because when I decided to believe in Miracles twenty-plus years ago and my new life as a Miracle Alchemist began, it was just a simple hope for a better life. Now, I not only Believe in Miracles and Receive Them, I have Miracles I never knew I wanted until the moment they arrive – finding me through people, places, and things I never could have imagined on my own. I have no doubt that you and I meeting here, in this book, is a Miracle, because I believe The Universe conspired to bring about our kismet encounter. So, take this as a sign that your Miracle is on its way, because nothing is by chance and...

"MIRACLES ARE EVERYWHERE, WAITING FOR AN OPPORTUNITY TO BE WITH YOU!"

Just keep talking to your Miracles as if they're a Dear Old Friend, and do the four steps suggested in each chapter. They will help you focus on what's important and distract you from what could possibly unconsciously be blocking your Miracles, and this will EXPEDITE YOUR MIRACLE LIFE! Please know that I have already prayed for this book to find everyone it was meant to and help them RECEIVE their Miracles SOONER. That means that just by holding this book in your hands, you've already received a Miracle!

It would be a Miracle to me if you gave a positive review for this book on Amazon, because reviews help this book reach more people, to help more people live their Miracle life.

Receive a FREE GIFT!

EVERY MONTH I draw a name from my EMAIL list and give away one of the following: A Miracle Reading; a Miracle Oracle Card deck; or a copy of one of my books with a personalized Miracle Message to you. **You have 12 opportunities a year to win!** Here's a link to be entered in my drawing and receive the latest news of my next book and monthly Miracle Messages.

Bit.ly/subscribeformiracles

With Gratitude and, As Always, Love & Miracle Wishes Sent Your Way,

Bernadette Rodebaugh

Continue the Miracle-Licious Transformation

*I*f you'd like to connect with BERNADETTE and talk or learn even more about Manifesting Miracles, here are various options.

ONLINE COURSE

Miracle Accelerator

If you're ready to elevate your Miracle Mindset and expedite your Miracle journey, then the "Miracle Accelerator" course is the perfect one for you! Bernadette has customized this course just for her readers to help them UNDERSTAND and RECEIVE CRYSTAL-CLEAR GUIDANCE FROM THEIR MIRACLES. Join here:

themiracle-school.com/p/miracle-accelerator

MENTORING

A Month of Miracle Strategy Mentoring

Do you wish Bernadette could help guide you personally to CALL IN your Miracles with an INTUITIVE STRATEGIC MIRACLE PLAN that helps remove the stress and overwhelm of trying to figure out "YOUR NEXT BEST STEP" toward your Miracle Life?

themiracle-ologist.com/miracle-mentoring-1

EVENTS

Bernadette loves speaking and presenting about Miracles – through workshops, summits, retreats, and interviews on all platforms. If you have a request for her to appear in your town or on your channel, please reach out to her at:

Miracles@bernadetterodebaugh.com

NEW BOOKS

Bernadette's upcoming book and cards *YOUR MIRACLE ANGELS,* and her *MIRACLE ANGEL ORACLE* cards are coming soon! Join her mailing list to stay notified of their release:

Bit.ly/subscribeformiracles

MIRACLE GUIDANCE TOOLS

Activate Your Miracle Guidance Cards

These cards can be used daily as Miracle Guidance Affirming cards or Oracle cards. They are designed to help you more easily receive Miracle Guidance by first ASKING a question to your

Higher Power, then, using your INNER GUIDANCE, flip over one or more cards to receive answers about your Miracle Message.

https://bit.ly/4d6T0KI

OTHER RESOURCES

Website: **themiracle-ologist.com**
Follow on Facebook: **Facebook.com/miracleologist**
Believe It To Receive It Facebook Group (personalized help to call in your Miracles): **Facebook.com/groups/believeittoreceiveit**
Connect on Instagram: **Instagram.com/themiracleologist**
Watch on TikTok: **@miracle_expert_author**

About the Author

$\mathcal{B}$ernadette Rodebaugh, also known as "The Miracle-ologist," began her career as an author only because she received persistent inner guidance that she couldn't deny, even though she had no writing experience or any ideas of what the book was supposed to be about. However, since she's a firm believer in following all Inner Guidance, she committed herself to writing weekly. Three months later, the book's subject revealed itself to her.

Bernadette continued writing for about two years; then, when the book was nearly done, she accidentally erased it! Only bits and pieces were able to be recovered. Bernadette lost her will to rewrite the book, so she began doing small workshops for entrepreneurs using her Miracles manifesting knowledge, her business education, and her certification from Myers-Briggs Type Indicator (MBTI) to assess personalities and communication styles.

After doing these workshops for about a year, Bernadette decided she was ready to write again. To her surprise, during that time off she had unknowingly already rewritten the new book from the weekly workbooks she created to help her clients. Her first book, *Believe It To Receive It: Activate The Miracles Waiting For You,* has been a number-one bestseller on Amazon so many times she has lost count; it has sold 11,000+ copies (and counting) around the world and received the 2024 International Impact Award.

Bernadette's career as an author has been filled with Miraculous Miracle opportunities, evidence that she lives and breathes what she teaches in her books, courses, and oracle cards. Currently, Bernadette resides in Colorado with her husband, son, and two rescued pit bulls

Acknowledgments

Mom and Dad,

I appreciate you for all the times I told you all about my big ideas and dreams and you never told me to be realistic or to dream smaller, even though my ideas seemed unimaginable to you. Instead, you allowed me to see the world as a miraculous place with endless possibilities, so I never knew my ideas were unconventional. THIS WAS THE BEGINNING OF ME BELIEVING IN MIRACLES AND BECOMING THE MIRACLE ALCHEMIST I WAS ALWAYS MEANT TO BE. Thank you!

Aunt Bena,

My second mom, you taught me about spirituality, metaphysics, religion, and rituals. Most importantly, when times are rough and I felt the world was against me, you showed me how to drop to my knees and talk to God and my angels and ask for guidance. This has helped me tremendously because even in the depths of my darkness when I felt alone, I knew I wasn't, because I had them and you...my earth angel!

My husband...my soulmate,

You are a true MIRACLE MAN, and the best spiritual teacher I've ever had (who is NOT spiritual). Thank you for your daily sacrifices; without you, these books would not be possible. You are my secret resource and component that helps me fulfill my life purpose: to be The Miracle-ologist I came into this life to be!

And last but certainly not least,

A heartfelt thank you to Transcendent Publishing, Shanda Trofe, and my amazing editor Dana Micheli. I'm so grateful for the love and care you've poured into helping me bring all my books to life, while staying true to my voice and vision. Sharing my heart and soul on paper, with complete transparency, is not always easy, but with your professional guidance, you make the process feel effortless. Thank you for sharing your life's purpose with me and the world!

Journal